ANYTHING
GOES

This book is dedicated to all my students. Thank you for teaching me.

ANYTHING GOES

PRACTICAL KARATE FOR THE STREETS

LOREN W. CHRISTENSEN

PALADIN PRESS
BOULDER, COLORADO

Also by Loren Christensen:

Skinhead Street Gangs

The Way Alone: Your Path to Excellence in the Martial Arts

The Way of the Warrior: The Violent Side

Winning with American Kata: The New Breed of Competitors

Anything Goes: Practical Karate for the Streets
by Loren W. Christensen

ISBN 0-87364-568-5
Printed in the United States of America

Published by Paladin Press, a division of
Paladin Enterprises, Inc., P.O. Box 1307,
Boulder, Colorado 80306, USA.
(303) 443-7250

Direct inquiries and/or orders to the above address.

Contents

 # Acknowledgments

Special thanks to my senior black belt, Gary Sussman, for his work behind the camera. Thanks to my students who posed: Amy Christensen, Dan Christensen, Gary Sussman, Scott Wong, Guy Wheat, Donna Pearson, Chau Vu, Bill Ramsour, and Tom Dietz.

Introduction

I haven't always been pragmatic in my study of the martial arts. I began training in 1965 in a Korean fighting system that was basic and somewhat unrealistic. The techniques were typical traditional "robot techniques" that were stiff, static, and impractical. Karate was in its infancy in the United States then and in my naiveté, I thought the style I was learning was the last answer in streetfighting.

As the number of karate tournaments increased toward the end of the 1960s, my instructor began to modify the style to fit the needs of sport karate. He was a genius at this, and soon we were the school to beat. By the early 1970s, we were a large chain, with many students and many sport karate champions. Indeed, we were full of pride and school spirit because we were winners.

I followed my instructor without question. I was taught that if I scored with a technique, I could have really hurt the guy if it were a real physical confrontation and I hadn't controlled the blow. It never occurred to me that there was a difference between sport fighting and streetfighting. I had only been in a few schoolyard fights as a youth, so my practical experience was limited.

1

I trained this way for two years. Most of the class time was spent sparring tournament style and the rest of the time was devoted to traditional kata. We continually reinforced each other with praise and were confident our techniques would be deadly should a street thug have the misfortune to pick on us.

In early 1967 I was promoted to brown belt and a few months later I joined the United States Army as a military policeman. I spent two years at various stateside duty stations, and I was able to practice on my own and teach a few soldiers what I had learned. I taught karate the only way I knew: move around, sneak in and tag a point, get away, and then stop and talk about the point.

While stationed in Florida, I was able to study a traditional Japanese style for awhile, but it was so stiff and unrealistic that its only value was as an exercise.

After four years of study, I didn't know much about the practical side of karate, but I didn't realize it. My primary concern was to get in and score, which is what I thought real fighting was all about.

In 1969 I was sent to Saigon, Vietnam, and was assigned to the 716th Military Police Battalion as a patrolman. The fun and games I enjoyed my first two years in the army suddenly came to an end.

Patrolling one of the roughest cities in the world brought the military police into contact with every undesirable element the war had to offer. Its streets, sidewalks, bars, massage parlors, and brothels were crowded with thieves, killers, beggars, prostitutes, dopers, con men, drunk American servicemen, and the Vietcong. It was a policeman's nightmare.

I was assigned to a walking beat consisting of four American military policemen, two Vietnamese military policemen, and two civilian Vietnamese policemen. Three of the American MPs were chosen because they were monsters. In fact, one had been a linebacker with the Chicago Bears. Although I was 5'11" and 200 pounds and the smallest American MP, I had been chosen because I was a brown belt in karate.

In spite of our number and the size of some of the officers, we got into a half dozen or more scuffles a night. Sometimes it was just a drunk soldier who stiffened his arms and refused to be escorted out of a bar. Other times it was a burned-out, freaked-out marine attacking everyone in sight with a bayonet.

Walking a beat in Saigon was the opportunity of a lifetime for a martial artist to test his skill and see what did and did not work. It didn't take long for me to realize that tournament tag was not going to help me at all. The first time I hit someone with a punch to the ribs, a blow that would have easily earned a point in a tournament, the guy just kept on fighting. The second guy I fought I hit with a hard and fast roundhouse kick; he staggered for a second and then leaped at me. I quickly learned that people in real fights can take a harder blow than tournament competitors. Most of the time the fights were nothing like karate sparring matches; they were explosive, far more violent, and over in a few seconds.

After the first week of patrolling the streets of Saigon, I decided that if I was to survive for a year, I was going to have to adjust my attitude about karate—mentally, physically, and philosophically.

Mentally, I had to clear my mind of sport karate and accept the fact I was in a war zone where the fighting was real and winning meant survival, not a plastic trophy. The "opponents" I would be confronting were not interested in scoring points on me; they were interested in hurting me and escaping.

Physically, my techniques had to be basic, simple, and executed hard and fast into vulnerable targets that would drop a person fast. I could no longer sneak in a fancy punch or kick, then stop and wait for the judges' approval. I had to move in with an explosive blitz to overwhelm the opponent and not stop until he either gave up or was no longer able to resist. I had to use grappling techniques and I had to think about the best way to use my nightstick.

I developed a survivor's personal philosophy. The army didn't pay me enough to get hit first before I could use physical force. As soon as my gut instinct told me a guy was going to resist, fight, or escape, I was going to move in and take him. The old saying "the best defense is a good offense" is a philosophy I used everyday in Vietnam and continue to use to this day. It has been a philosophy that has displeased a lot of people, especially my opponents. But as a policeman since 1967 and countless physical confrontations later, I have been hit only once by surprise.

When I returned home in 1970, I decided I would no longer train in sport karate. I had come face-to-face with extraordinary violence in Vietnam and my adjustments in the three areas had paid off. Sometimes I was a little ragged after a confrontation, but not as bad as I would have been had I continued to tournament-tag my way through fights. From then on, I decided, I would always strive to make my training as realistic as possible. To this day, I have continued to study and teach realistically and to stay true to the original premise of self-defense in the martial arts.

I am not completely against sport karate. It can help develop timing, explosiveness, and courage. It is also a place where a student can learn new techniques, make friends, and develop a fighting spirit.

Although these are positive attributes, all too often competitors allow the negative elements to overshadow them. Excessive ego, trophy hunting, unrealistic techniques and concepts, and false confidence are all negative attributes of tournament competition that will lead to failure in a street self-defense situation.

If you train only for competition, these elements are virtually impossible to avoid. In fact, this situation is particularly dangerous because many competitors today develop the negatives and then are unaware of them. They assume that because they can earn a point, they will be victorious in a streetfight. Maybe, but probably not.

I have seen streetfighters who have never set foot in a martial arts school but could give any of our nationally ranked competitors a tough fight. Many of these people have spent years fighting on the street and have learned from the school of hard experience what it takes to survive. They are tough enough to take your point-getting, weak, flip-up head kick and drive a knife into your thigh for your troubles. They don't care about your belt rank, but they do care about your money, and if they have to hurt you to get it, so be it. There are a lot of tournament fighters who have already had this experience. Some will admit it, but most won't.

Tournament competition is steadily growing in popularity. Students are clamoring after trophies, cash prizes, and recognition. Along the way, however, they forget the original premise of the martial arts. What is the value of a room full of trophies and your face on the cover of a karate magazine if your fighting techniques are of questionable value in a real violent situation?

This book examines tournament techniques and concepts from the standpoint of street effectiveness. Although you may be surprised to learn that many of your favorite point techniques are worthless out of the ring, you will learn variations that will make them effective. You will learn how to change your mind-set from sport competition to street-fighting and how you can effectively combine the two. You will learn how to make your hands and feet more effective for the street, and you will be provided with a variety of exercises to make sparring more realistic. You will be made more aware of your environment and learn how you can use it to your advantage and to your attacker's disadvantage. You will learn about close fighting, a place where tournament fighters are weak but where most real fights occur.

Many tournament fighters close their ears to those who argue that much of sport karate is ineffective against a tough streetfighter. Fame, trophies, and money are powerful lures that will close a competitor's ears to everything but what he wants to hear. Approach this book with open ears and an open mind. It is not an argument against competition.

You can still compete, but you must also train for the street. You can combine the two, but only if you can accept the fact that they are different.

This book will help you see the difference.

1 Changing Your Thinking

A phrase repeated frequently throughout this text is: "How you train is how you will react in a real fight." If you train only for karate tournaments, you will naturally use sport karate in a self-defense situation. Common sense should tell you this is true, although most karate competitors will deny it adamantly. They are convinced they will be able to change their sport techniques to streetfighting techniques instantly.

This will not happen.

LEARNING THE HARD WAY

I have seen countless examples of people responding in a real situation the same way they have trained. There is the story of a policeman, Officer Adams, who was fascinated with practicing disarming techniques against someone holding him at gunpoint. He spent hours having a training partner point a gun at him. He would then respond by raising his hands in submission, twisting his body away, slapping the gun to the side, and then executing a flawless wristlock takedown. Officer Adams would then hand the gun back to his training partner and repeat the drill over and over again.

Sometime after he had mastered this skill, he and a partner

received a radio call to a convenience store on a "suspicious person on the premises." When they got to the store, the clerk described a man who had been acting strangely and was now walking around the aisles. Officer Adams and his partner split up to look for him.

As Officer Adams rounded the end of an aisle, he was confronted by a man pointing a gun at his chest. In the blink of an eye, the officer twisted his body out of the line of fire, swatted the gun aside, and slammed the suspect to the floor with a perfectly executed wristlock. Then, just as he had done in training hundreds of times, Officer Adams handed the gun back.

Officer Adams immediately realized his mistake as the suspect scooted out of reach and pointed the weapon at the officer's head. Fortunately, Adams' partner approached from another aisle, shot the suspect, and saved Officer Adams' life.

Although the act of handing the gun back to the suspect was certainly not in the officer's best interest, it was a reaction based on his training. How you train is how you will react in a real situation.

DON'T POINT

In the police academy, we teach officers the mechanics of holding a suspect at gunpoint. They are shown how to make a suspect lie on his belly and then how to search and handcuff him. We used to tell the officers to simulate a weapon with their fingers as they practiced the exercises in the classroom. A problem arose, however, when we moved on to practicing arrest situations outside, in full uniform and with real but inoperable guns. Although they were permitted to use their weapons, many officers had developed a habit of simulating a firearm with their fingers.

We immediately stopped using fingers in the classroom exercises and provided the officers with inoperable guns in all phases of the training. It was fortunate that we learned while still in training that how you practice is how you will react in a real situation.

This student is creating a bad habit. He blocks . . .

HOW YOU TRAIN IS HOW YOU WILL COMPETE

Since my karate school trains for the street, we emphasize kicking an opponent's leg muscles and joints, punching the throat, gouging the eyes, breaking limbs, pulling hair, and an assortment of other nasties. When some of my students want to compete in a tournament, they must change their training, mentally and physically. I discovered a long time ago that if their training isn't modified at least three weeks prior to the event, they will compete the same way they had practiced in class, which results in their immediate

. . . disarms . . .

disqualification.

We also practice the Filipino stick-fighting art of arnis. When practicing disarming techniques, the students used to, out of courtesy, pick up their partner's stick. Then, in the heat of an arnis sparring match, students would run around picking up sticks instead of moving in for a finishing technique. How you train . . . you're probably getting the idea by now.

REAL FIGHTING IS NOT A GAME OF TAG

Is sport karate effective in a real situation? This question has been debated in the karate magazines for years. Karate

. . . and routinely hands the knife back to his opponent.

people who have used their art to survive in the tough streets of any large American city will answer "no." Most people involved in the sport, however, will answer "yes."

My answer is based on having been a police officer since 1967, a profession that has exposed me, as a participant and witness, to countless fights and physical assaults. My answer is that with few exceptions, sport karate is not effective in the street and, in fact, can be detrimental. The exceptions are those few competitors who possess incredible power, speed, fighting spirit, and fighting savvy. They would fare better on the street than the average tournament competitor, but there are few of them. For reasons we will examine later, even these rare individuals could have problems.

To do well in the street, you must train and think in terms of realism and practicality. You must clear your mind of the concept of sport karate, a concept that reduces the ancient fighting art to a fancy game of tag. Tournament fighting is a game of strategy and physical skill, both of which can be quite complex. But complexity does not make it any more effective for the street. In fact, the more complex a movement or concept is, the greater the chance that it will not be effective in a real fight.

BEGIN BY EXAMINING YOUR REPERTOIRE

You must begin to examine your repertoire of tournament techniques to determine how effective they really are. Effectiveness should be measured in terms of *stopping power* rather than a technique's ability to score. Ask yourself: "Will this fancy kick drop an opponent? Will this sneaky punch to the midsection really stop someone bent on hurting me?" Examine the way you move, your stances, and how you react after you have scored a point (that's a big problem, which we will discuss later).

Whether your motivation is to change your system, completely modify your fighting style, or just include more streetfighting in your training, your first step is to stop thinking about sport and begin thinking about the street. You must be analytical, suspicious of unproven techniques and concepts, thorough in your approach, and (this is the hard part) be willing to admit you have held some false beliefs.

MULTIPLE HITS VERSUS THE SINGLE POINT

In the late 1960s and early 1970s, all tournament judges had to give a quick demonstration of the competitor's technique that they thought had scored. If one judge demonstrated a punch and another called a side kick, no point was rewarded because there was no agreement. This practice was probably a product of traditional Japanese karate that

A punch to the midsection is a good technique in a tournament, but will it stop someone wearing a heavy winter coat?

emphasized the so-called "one-point kill" technique.

The old way created one-technique tournament fighters. Such concepts as exaggerating techniques to make them more visible and being cognizant of where the judges were standing were critical factors to getting the technique seen by as many judges as possible. Combination techniques were rare because the judges might not agree on which technique scored. This destroyed any sense of realism in the sport and encouraged the concept of tag karate.

It's a little better today because most tournaments do not require that judges agree on which technique scored, an improvement that encourages multiple strikes. If you move in with a roundhouse kick, reverse punch, and backfist, then move out of range with another roundhouse kick, you will have a better chance of getting a point from the judges. One judge sees your first roundhouse, another judge sees the backfist, and the referee sees your last roundhouse. They all see something different but you get the point anyway.

Although multiple strikes earn points, the majority of tournament fighters still think in terms of the single hit. This is unfortunate because multiple hitting is a step in the right direction toward making tournament fighting a little more realistic.

THE SINGLE-HIT MYTH

One of the first hard lessons I learned on the street was that most fights require hitting an adversary more than once, whether it's with a fist or a foot. There have been a few times when I have seemingly just tapped someone and they have fallen down, but those times have been rare. Most often it has taken two or more techniques to get the job done.

Many karate people walk around believing they have dynamite sticks for hands and pile drivers for feet. This may be true, but most of the time it's going to take several sticks of dynamite and several pile-driving kicks to get the job done. Street situations rarely provide ideal environments and conditions. You may have to contend with such negative factors

In competition, a single technique that misses doesn't matter . . .

as rough terrain, slippery floors, tight clothing, crowded spaces, or distractions. Your attacker may be intoxicated or mentally ill, have a high pain threshold, or be wearing heavy clothing.

My own personal philosophy on self-defense is that if I have exhausted all ways to avoid the fight and the situation has gotten to the point where I have to resort to physical technique, I am going to attack until the attacker either submits or is down and can no longer continue. I certainly am not going to hit him once and then step back to watch

... but in a streetfight it may make the attacker more intent on getting you.

his reaction. What if he doesn't react and rushes in and beats me up? Since I do not want to give him that opportunity, I will hit him with multiple techniques.

To reiterate, you may have extraordinary power and have sent the needle on an impact gauge into the red. Those blows, however, were tested under conditions that allowed you to hit with perfect form, balance, footwork, and distancing. Since the street rarely provides you with these ideal circumstances, why take the chance and depend on one hit to do the job?

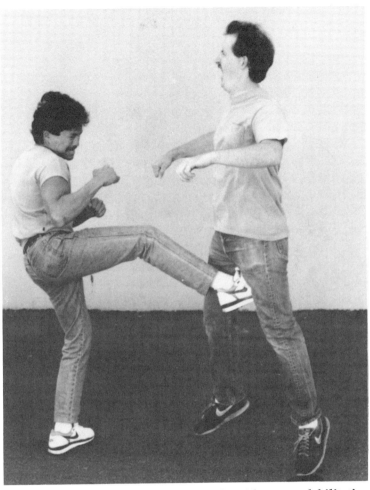

This streetfighter will follow through with *more* debilitating techniques rather than relying on just one.

TOURNAMENT RULES VERSUS THE STREET RULE

A tournament, because it's a game, has rules. Without rules the game would be chaos and there would be many injuries. Rules, like traffic laws, work to maintain control, order, discipline, and safety. They provide everyone with the same guidelines as to what they can and cannot do.

It's important for tournament fighters to understand the rules and abide by them. They must continually keep them in the forefront of their minds as they train and compete.

A stomp on a bridged knee will break the rules in a tournament. In the street, where there are no rules, it will break a leg.

To disobey the rules risks injury to the opponent, which means disqualification, forfeiture of the entry fee, and a waste of training, time, and travel.

Common questions tournament fighters ask when they hear about an upcoming tournament are: "What are the rules? Do they allow groin kicks? Can I score with a hit to the back? Will it be two- or three-minute rounds? Are two points awarded for head kicks?" Knowing the rules is important in order to know how to play the game.

Experienced competitors learn to use the rules to their

advantage. They will dance around the ring when they are ahead on points to allow the time to run out. They will throw techniques that can be seen on the side exposed to two judges rather than the side where only one can see. When competing out of town, they will throw specific techniques they know are popular in that area.

In tournament karate, you go to the arena with the intent of fighting; you do not try to get out of it and, in fact, you pay money to do it. Part of the attraction is that you know it is a game and you know you will not get hurt to any significant degree. You compete knowing there are rules that help maintain safety and the concept of sport.

Although there are many rules in tournament karate, the only rule on the street is *there are no rules*. Anything goes, because real fighting is not sport and it is definitely not a game of tag. The attacker wants to hurt you, perhaps take your possessions. He may even want to kill you.

PREREQUISITES TO THROWING OUT THE RULES

I give my students five prerequisites to consider before they get into a real fight:

1. If you have an avenue of escape, use it and run.
2. Use your brain and mouth and try to talk your way out of it.
3. If you can't run, block the attack and use a restraint hold.
4. If you can't use a restraint hold, then use the least amount of karate you can to get the job done.
5. If all the above fail to do the job, then do what you have to do to win.

HOW YOU TRAIN . . .

The competitor has practiced in accordance with strict guidelines that determine the amount of space he can fight in, a set time frame in which he fights, a small number of targets he can hit, and a general sense that there are only a limited number of offensive and defensive techniques he can use.

How you train is how you will fight in a real situation. There is a strong possibility that when confronted by an assailant armed with a screwdriver, the tournament competitor will block the weapon and snap-punch the attacker in the ribs as if he were scoring a point. The karate student whose roots are in streetfighting will react by gaining control of the weapon hand, slapping the attacker across the eyes to distract him, and taking him to the ground using an arm or wristlock. He will then apply more pressure through the lock and kick the man in the ribs to assist in the removal of the weapon.

The difference between these two students is the type of training they have experienced mentally and physically. The competitor's training has been directed towards earning a point and obeying all of the tournament rules. The other student has trained to survive a self-defense situation; he doesn't think about restrictions but about all the things he can do to survive.

IT'S NEVER TOO LATE TO CHANGE

How sad it would be, not to mention embarrassing, to train for many years in sport karate and then get creamed in a street confrontation. Unfortunately, this has happened far too many times. If your training has been directed primarily toward sport, you can lessen the chance of this happening by modifying the way you train and think right now.

It's important that you read through this book and consider the arguments against training solely for competition. It's easy to read a section and say, "That's not me. I don't have those problems." It's paramount that you be honest with yourself and admit that you can see yourself in many, if not most, of the examples. Once you can admit that, then you are on your way to being a karate student who is effective in the ring and has a better chance of surviving a street situation.

FIRST, CHANGE YOUR THINKING

Your first step is to change your way of thinking about

karate. You must look at karate as more than just earning points and winning trophies. You must begin to think of it as it was intended — as a means of survival.

Survival was the original premise behind the development of the martial arts and it is still important today, especially when you consider the crime situation on our city streets. It is quite possible your skill in karate may save you or a loved one from injury or death. Can you imagine how you would feel if someone you cared for was hurt because your sport karate was ineffective?

As a military policeman in Vietnam, I quickly realized that my tournament techniques were not going to help me. It took only two or three days of dealing with all kinds of violent people to decide I had to change my thinking from sport-fighting techniques to ones that would save my rear.

I no longer could think in terms of flashy, fun techniques that would thrill a crowd and get the judges to award me a point. I had to learn how to deal with a drunk 225-pound marine swinging a bar stool at me. I had to think how to defend against a 19-year-old deserter who had led me on an exhausting foot chase down several streets and alleys and over rooftops and then fought like a wild animal when cornered. I had to figure out how to fight an enraged Green Beret who had no neck, a chest as big as a fifty-gallon barrel, and arms the size of army jeeps.

Once I made the switch mentally and changed my way of training, I was more confident and successful in my job. With my mind on survival, I was able to sense potential threats more quickly and I was able to diffuse many situations before they became physical.

There are two ways you can make a change. You can change your tournament style to one that is completely street oriented or you can change to a style that is a combination of both street and sport. The latter is the most difficult, but it can be done. The change begins with your mental approach.

Your thinking must now be in terms of fighting to survive. You must know how to weaken an assailant through the use of control techniques applied to vulnerable targets. If the situation requires more force, you must think in terms of stopping the assailant with techniques that inflict debilitating injury. If the situation is one of life and death, you must think in terms of maximum — or deadly — force against the attacker.

LOTS OF TARGETS

Start thinking about targets that are never hit in competition. Keep in mind that they are considered nontargets because of their potential for injury. If a poorly controlled blow can cause injury to these targets, imagine what a deliberate and full-powered blow can do.

In my school, every part of the body is considered a target. We claw the eyes, slap the ears, elbow the base of the brain, cram fingers up the nose, strike the throat with the forearm, claw the nipples, stomp the ribs, kick the butt, kick the groin with the shins, attack the muscles and joints of the legs, kick the ankle bones, and stomp on the feet. Practicing for a real fight should include everything.

There are so many more good targets than just those allowed in competition. In chapter six we will look at the physiological results of striking various targets without protective hand and foot gear. It is amazing how vulnerable these targets are when struck with full-power karate techniques.

COMBINING STREET AND SPORT TRAINING

The focus of training in my school is surviving a street confrontation. People join my school because they are not interested in sport karate but want to train in a style that is oriented toward realistic situations. On occasion, however, there will be a few students who want to fight in an upcoming tournament. I give permission only if I know they have a clear understanding of the differences between the two concepts.

Even though they understand, they must modify their training to accommodate the two different approaches to fighting. Since it takes three to four weeks for most people to make the mental and physical change, it is necessary to plan in advance.

I begin their modified training by having the tournament competitors work together when they spar. Since they need to practice tournament techniques, I don't want them to "infect" the other students, who are training for the street.

The competitors then practice tournament-style sparring, meaning they no longer can kick legs, gouge eyes, and grapple when their opponent is down. They need to think in terms of fighting within a ring, being more cautious with their control, playing to the judges, employing popular tournament techniques, using tournament strategy, and so on. I continually tell them they are training for a game and, for the most part, the techniques they are using are sport techniques and may or may not be effective in a real fight. I never want them to lose sight of that fact.

The Monday following the tournament, they resume their training for the street. The problem is not so much getting them to resume thinking about the street but rather getting them to discontinue their tournament style. It's amazing how quickly a person can slip into the habit of sport karate.

Although I don't encourage tournament competition, I don't discourage it either. I try to give students what they want out of their study, as long as it fits in with the basic premise of the school. I do make it clear, however, that a student who wants to train for sport must continue to train for the street, with an emphasis on the latter. If the student spars tournament-style in class when there is not an upcoming tournament, I make him change immediately. If he spars tournament-style during a test, he flunks. I will not change my philosophy because someone is paying mc dues.

Training for both the street and tournaments will work only if the emphasis is on the street. If you wanted to enter a tournament every week, it wouldn't work because your emphasis would primarily be on competitive sparring. If you competed in four tournaments a year and trained three weeks before each one, you would spend twelve weeks a year training for sport and forty weeks training for the street. This would be a workable formula only if the tournaments were spread evenly throughout the year. Any more than this and you would be risking training too much for the game.

BEFORE YOU CAN CHANGE, YOU NEED TO KNOW THE DIFFERENCE

To change your way of thinking about streetfighting and tournament fighting, you must first *believe* there is a difference. Some tournament competitors will not change because they won't admit that their training may not work on an attacker who is really trying to hurt them.

There are also competitors who do not want to change because they don't care about self-defense, preferring to train solely for sport. This is fine as long as they don't get overconfident about their abilities in a real confrontation. I know a top-rated competitor who freely admits that he would have trouble in a tough streetfight. He is retiring soon and plans to change his entire training approach to one of realistic self-defense. It's never too late to change.

If you have been in a tournament mode for a long time and you want to make the change, this book will get you going in the right direction.

2 Hand Techniques

A LOOK AT THE REVERSE PUNCH

Most fighting styles use a technique commonly called the reverse punch, a straight punch executed with the rear hand. For example, if you were in a fighting stance with your left leg forward, your right hand would be used to reverse punch.

It is the staple hand technique among tournament fighters, with the backfist running a close second. It is popular because it is an easy technique to use no matter what position you or your opponent may be in. The most important reason for its popularity, however, is that judges like to award points for good, solid reverse punches.

Reverse punching is so popular that many matches are boring because that is all the competitors do. Although it isn't a flashy technique and it doesn't thrill audiences the way a perfectly executed head kick does, the reverse punch can be a sneaky, versatile technique that can slip into the tiniest opening and garner that all-important point.

The kamikaze reverse punch

In the last few years, many tournament competitors have used a method of delivery I call the kamikaze reverse punch.

A reverse punch from the beginning position . . .

. . . to the completed position.

The kamikaze punch is thrown with the arm fully extended, the body stretched out, and the rear leg frequently airborne.

The kamikaze were Japanese pilots who deliberately crashed their planes into American warships, knowing they would die in the process.

The kamikaze reverse punch is launched with the punching arm extended ahead of the charging body, similar to a battering ram. The head is held down, so the punch is often thrown blindly. Some competitors are quite good at this technique and have earned many points and many championships as a result.

The reverse punch as a self-defense technique

Is the reverse punch a good technique to use in the street? The answer is simple: it depends. To elaborate, let's briefly examine the structure of the punch.

The fingers are curled into a fist and the thumb is either pressed against the index finger or placed across the index and middle fingers. The primary striking surface is made up of the knuckles of the index and middle fingers. The back of the hand is held flat and flush with the wrist. Traditionally, the fist is launched from the ribs, palm up, along a straight line to the target, and then rotates to palm down just short of impact.

Although the reverse punch is one of the first techniques taught to beginners, it takes time to gain proficiency and even longer to gain mastery. Nevertheless, with three or four months of training, white belts enter tournaments and use the technique to slug away at each other. An educated guess is that if the average white belt throws ten reverse punches in a match, half of them are executed incorrectly. Although the percentage for error will be less as the belt rank goes up, in many cases it will still be high enough to be of concern.

Why?

The typical competitor is concerned more with getting the punch in to score than holding the fist properly. This is okay as long as the student continues to train to master the technique. But will he? Or will winning points and a trophy dominate his thinking and convince the student that what he is doing is correct?

As a long-time tournament judge, I have seen competitors with terrible technique but good ring savvy win over fighters with good technique but poor ring savvy over and over again. The poor technician will bounce around in elation, believing that what he did must have been correct because he was awarded a point for it. Inevitably, I will see the same person at a tournament months later and he will still be fighting with sloppy technique.

The tournament system gives the student positive re-inforcement for poor technique. Sadly, many teachers will not make the winning student return to basics for fear of upsetting the student's ego, upsetting his winning method, or losing him to another school.

If this student has earned a lot of points and won a lot of matches with a reverse punch, as sloppy as it is, his wins, his attitude about his wins, and the disservice caused by his instructor's silence have aided in the creation of a weak punching foundation. This could create a serious problem

Earning a point for a sloppy punch reinforces bad technique.

if he had to rely on his punch in a self-defense situation.

Look at some of the tournament photos in the karate magazines. Many of them show the puncher with his back leg up in the air, his body leaning forward awkwardly, the arm overextended, and the wrist bent. The photo caption says that so-and-so received a point for this technique. In a real fight, however, if the puncher had made hard contact with his blow, he would have injured his wrist or knuckles, and his overextended reach and weak foundation would have resulted in a loss of balance. A good streetfighter would take full advantage of these problems.

Injury to the knuckles occurs frequently in real fights.

"Boxer's fracture" is a term used by doctors to describe damage to the knuckle of the little finger, a common form of hand trauma received by fighters. Little-knuckle injuries and sprained wrists are direct results of holding the hand improperly when punching.

Keep in mind that how you practice and compete will determine how you will react in a real fight. If you have been punching sloppily in tournaments but you believe that in a streetfight you will suddenly hold your hand correctly, you are in for a rude awakening.

You can't continue to ignore the fact that competition can reinforce poor technique. Trophies are awarded for tagging an opponent, not because techniques are delivered flawlessly. Once you have accepted this fact, and for some people the intoxication of winning makes this difficult, you will have taken a big step toward improving your technique.

No matter how many tournaments you win, continue to work on mastering the reverse punch. Japanese masters say that it is a basic technique that takes a lifetime to perfect. Continue to practice the reverse punch and you will be armed with an even better technique for competition as well as an effective weapon to use in a street confrontation.

The reverse punch target

How many TV programs and movies have you seen where a man punches another man in the jaw and the puncher never even glances at his hand afterwards? The reality, however, is that punching someone in the jaw has the potential of hurting the hand, even when the hand is held correctly.

The entire head consists of bone, and the surface is uneven, especially around the face. There is the hollow of the cheek, the protrusions around the eyebrows, the raised surface of the forehead, and the horseshoe-shaped ridge of the jawline. These surfaces present an entirely different target than the comparatively soft, smooth surface of a punching bag. No matter how carefully you hold your fist when making contact on an uneven surface, your hand will give in the direction of the least resistance and be vulnerable to injury.

As a beginner, you are told to strike with the index and middle knuckles. Have you noticed that when you punch the heavy bag without gloves, all of your knuckles, including the area of the fingers between the striking knuckles and middle joints of the fingers, get red and sometimes skinned? No matter how accurately you punch, a surface with any kind of give will automatically involve a larger surface of your fist. This increases the likelihood of injury to your hand, especially if the surface is hard.

The head is not the best place to hit with a reverse punch because you never know what the result will be. Several years ago, I hit an armed robber in the face with a medium-power reverse punch. It broke his cheekbone, caused a cut deep enough to require eight stitches, and knocked him unconscious for nearly a minute. Amazingly, I didn't get a scratch

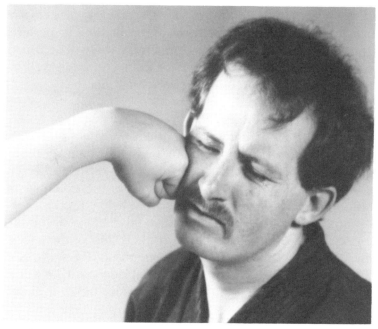

Punching the face may injure the hand.

on my hand. On another occasion, I punched a combative escaped prisoner behind his ear. It caused him only minor discomfort but shattered the knuckle of my little finger. Another time, I punched a man several times in the face while he was lying on his back with his head braced against the floor. My punches didn't phase him and he continued to fight like a man possessed.

If you insist on reverse punching to the head

Consider the side of the head, covering the area two or three inches on either side of the ear. This area is relatively smooth, so there is less chance the wrist will bend and a greater chance the two large knuckles will be the only knuckles to make contact. There is still the issue of the hard surface, but through training you can condition your hand and wrist to absorb considerable impact.

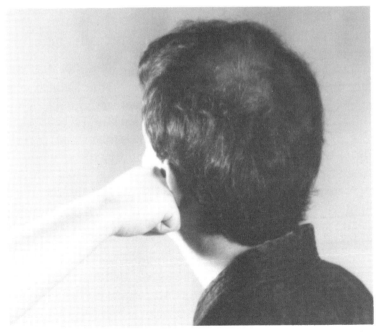

If you are going to punch the head, aim for the area around the ear.

You can develop good hand strength by exercising with weights. Perform exercises that strengthen the forearms, thicken the wrists and fingers, and develop a powerful grip. Supplement the weight exercises with push-ups on your index and middle knuckles.

In addition, you need to practice punching hard surfaces, such as the Japanese *makiwara* board. This device consists of an eight-foot two-by-four that is buried about four feet into the ground. The top twelve inches are beveled so the board gives when it is hit. Cover the top with whatever you want, but work up to a fairly hard covering. I have used a hard-packed bag of rice, a bag of sand, and sometimes I would wrap the top eight or nine inches with rope. The *makiwara* may be ancient, but it is still a great tool for developing tough knuckles and strong wrists.

Even with this training, the uneven surface of the face still presents a risk. It may be prudent, therefore, to use a different strike.

Some options to the reverse punch

The backfist is an excellent technique to use against the face because the wrist doesn't support it the same way it supports a reverse punch. Since the two large knuckles are the common point of impact with the backfist, there is some risk of injury when you strike a bony surface. But overall, the uneven surface is not as significant a factor as with the reverse punch.

Snap your hand forward so the two large knuckles make contact with the target. Be careful not to strike the ridge of the jaw with the back of your hand, where the bones are quite fragile.

The palm-heel strike is a good technique, but it is underrated and seldom used. It works well against the head because it's supported by the wrist and forearm. Since the heel is well padded, there is little chance of injury, even when striking the jaw. Make sure you bend your hand back enough so your fingers are out of the way upon impact.

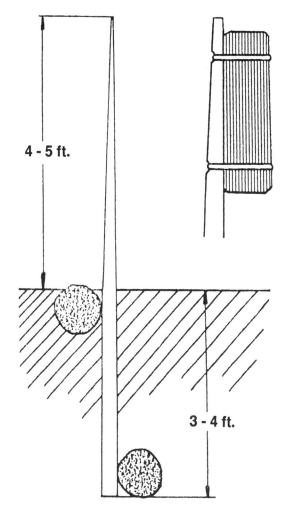

Get a seven- or eight-foot long 4x4 board and bevel the top four feet of one end so the very end is about a half-inch thick. Dig a hole in the ground three or four feet deep and plant the unbeveled end of the board. The top should be about as high as your upper chest. Fill the hole with large and small rocks. It's even better if you can cement it into the ground. The top of the board should be flexible enough to move five or six inches. It is better to have it a little loose rather than too tight. Fasten your striking pad so it covers the top twelve inches. The striking surface should be as high as your solar plexus.

A backfist is supported more firmly by the wrist and may be a better weapon to use against the face than a standard punch.

The palm-heel strike is a strong weapon because it is supported by the wrist and forearm.

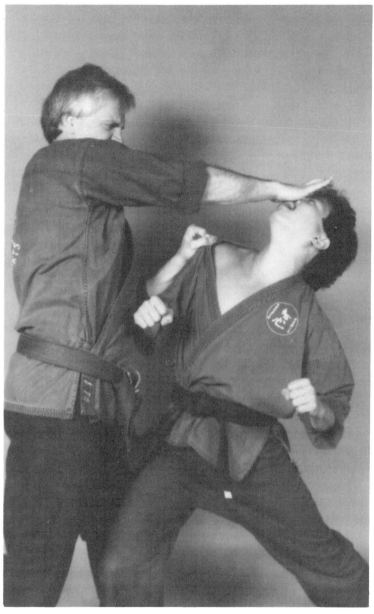

Slapping the face is a powerful strike with little risk of injury to the hand.

The slap is another underrated technique that can be quite devastating and is a relatively safe weapon to use against the face. You can use the lead or rear hand, depending on the circumstances.

When the slap is executed with the lead hand, the arm is extended toward the attacker's face in the same manner as a backfist. The hand is open and the wrist rotates so the impact is made with the palm and fingers. The lead hand is not as powerful as the rear hand, but it is quick and can be used to provide an element of surprise. When it is used against the nose, ear, or across the eyes, it is distracting and has the psychological effect of stunning an assailant long enough for you to flee or follow up with additional techniques.

The rear-hand slap can be executed with enough power to knock your opponent unconscious. It travels along the same route as a roundhouse punch. You snap the hips forward as the arm arcs toward the target, your hand open. If the attacker is a short distance away, lunge forward as you would with a punch and tense your muscles on impact. Try it on a bag and you will be pleasantly surprised at how powerful it is.

DIVING WITH THE BACKFIST AND RIDGEHAND

The diving backfist and diving ridgehand are similar to the kamikaze punch previously discussed. They are especially applicable for tournaments because they are flashy, catch the judges' attention, and can garner a lot of points. Some competitors execute them quite accurately and with enough power to actually hurt someone. Most, however, do not.

The diving backfist and ridgehand strikes are delivered from an explosive lunge, often executed with the head held down so as not to get hit. It is important that the lunge is executed as quickly as possible so there is an element of surprise and the opponent is overwhelmed by the charging body. Timing the lunge is essential, although many times the competitor will throw the technique with complete disregard for anything the opponent is doing.

Proper stances are often nonexistent, especially at the

The diving backfist, although sloppy and risky, frequently earns tournament points.

conclusion of the lunge. Sometimes the techniques are executed with the rear foot dragging behind uselessly or other times suspended in midair, a result of the forward momentum of the overextended lunge. Some competitors lunge with no intention of stopping after delivering the technique and run past the opponent and out of the ring.

To determine the effectiveness of diving techniques, you would have to evaluate each situation. Some diving backfists and ridgehand strikes land with good power, as attested to by those competitors who have had their brains jarred by them. Other times, especially with the backfist dives, the techniques land with all the impact of a powder puff.

Powder-puff techniques are a result of the attacking arm being fully extended long before the aggressor is close enough to the target. This results in a lunging push, a worthless technique by which many judges are fooled. When the aggressor launches his body with great explosiveness and accompanies the move with a shout, the powder-puff technique takes on the illusion of being very powerful, resulting in cheering crowds and judges awarding points.

Admittedly, the two techniques are interesting to watch in competition. There is an element of flash because they need to be executed explosively in order to score. Audiences like them, especially when the contact is hard enough to make a loud noise. Many of the big names have virtually built their reputations on them. It's safe to say that the techniques will be around for a long time.

But are these techniques effective in a real fight?

A good answer is that it depends on how they are used. A better answer is that the potential for problems with them is so great that it would be risky to use them.

One consideration is balance. If you were to execute a typical diving backfist, your arm would be fully extended, your body would be leaning out awkwardly, and your stance would be weak, if you used any stance at all. You will have fully committed yourself to the technique. This is a poor position to be in even for the best fighter because there is always the chance that your technique will miss or be blocked.

Most tournament fighters overcommit with the diving backfist and rarely follow the movement with other techniques. In a street situation, where pain tolerance is high, you must think in terms of multiple strikes. Never count on your diving backfist or any other single technique to end a fight.

Sometimes the diving backfist is executed with a run, which makes follow-up techniques impossible. It is important that you are able to control your techniques and your body at all times. If you find you are unable to follow up with something else, then you should eliminate the technique from your repertoire.

Check to see if you leave yourself open to punishment

when lunging. Keep in mind that a good streetfighter will not be reacting in the stylized methods used by most karate competitors. A streetfighter with basic boxing skills will bob and weave away from your backfist's trajectory and counter with hard body punches.

The diving ridgehand strike leaves you open more than the backfist because the strike is delivered with a large arc. If a good streetfighter sees it, your ribs are open season to him. To provide some protection, you should keep your opposite hand next to your chest.

The ridgehand is a good technique that delivers a lot of power, especially when used against a vulnerable target such

Throw a diving backfist on the street and you may get a knife in the ribs.

as the neck, cheek, ear, or nose. Executed from a dive against a streetfighter, however, may be more risk than you should take.

THE VICTORY FIST

One of my personal pet peeves with some tournament competitors is a little piece of business I call "the victory fist." The first time I saw it done in competition in the early 1970s, I was thoroughly disgusted, and my opinion hasn't changed. I guess it rubs directly against my belief that karate sparring, in a tournament or school, should have some semblance of realism.

The victory fist looks something like this: Bill and Kathy

This may sound absurd, but it has happened. The tournament fighter punches an assailant on the street . . .

are sparring. Bill sees an opening and hits it before Kathy can block. So far, so good, but now it gets stupid. Bill lets out a yelp, raises his fist in the air, turns his back on Kathy, and does a funny little walk back to his starting position. He looks a little like a professional football player after scoring a touchdown.

Sometimes Bill goes even further. After he yelps and raises his fist in the air, he makes an exaggerated motion of licking his index finger and gesturing as if he were keeping tally in the air, signifying he has scored a point.

The purpose of this foolishness is to draw attention to the technique and to sway the judges into awarding a point. I've

. . . and then raises his fist in victory.

seen competitors go through this routine even when their technique was blocked or had missed the target. Justice prevails when a competitor is so caught up in his victory dance that he doesn't realize the judges haven't called his point and the opponent scores on him.

These antics make karate look ridiculous. I've seen first-time spectators laugh uproariously at this foolishness. Is this how you want your art to be perceived?

Besides presenting an unfavorable image, the victory fist will create an undesirable habit. Imagine that a street punk has thrown a punch at you. You block it easily, tag him with a punch to the ribs, and then let out a victory yelp as you raise your fist high about your head, just as you have done many times in the school and in tournaments. Your attacker is either going to die laughing or take advantage of your foolishness and beat you to a pulp.

If you think it won't happen in a real fight after you have made a habit of it in practice and competition, you are only deluding yourself. I have heard competitors admit that it has happened to them on the street. How you practice is how you will react in a real fight. If you are doing this, you need to stop it now. It can cost you a match and it can get you hurt on the street.

SINGLE VS. MULTIPLE STRIKES

Although in competition you are allowed to attack with multiple techniques, most fighters try to score with only one. They move around and launch a front kick. When that gets blocked, they try a backfist. They continue in this fashion until one or the other gets a point.

You can walk around all day and tell yourself that your fists are kegs of dynamite, but the reality is you will most likely have to hit a real attacker more than once — probably several times.

Is this because you are weak? Maybe. But even if you possess incredible strength, there are a lot of people out there who can take a hard punch. The reasons for this are many:

they might be impervious to pain because they are high on alcohol or drugs, they are mentally deranged and their brains are unable to register the pain, your hand technique might have missed a vulnerable target and hit where it had little or no effect, or you may have put less power into the blow than you thought because you were using insufficient body mechanics in the movement. Since there are many reasons your single technique may fail to drop an attacker, you should play it safe and hit him several times from the outset.

Think in terms of combinations. As you spar, make a point of attacking in multiples and countering in multiples. The possibilities are many: hand/hand, foot/foot, hand/foot, and foot/hand are the foundation of double hits. You increase the possibilities when you add a third technique, and you increase them even more when you add a fourth.

Not every blow needs to be a knockout blow. But as you spar, keep in mind that in a real fight every blow should have some kind of an effect on the attacker, if only to distract his attention. Let's say you are sparring and there is a moment where your front foot is about six inches from your opponent's lead foot. As you begin your backfist, hit his ankle with your foot. This is a quick movement, with no power and no intention of causing any damage. Its purpose is to draw his attention down so that you can lunge in with a backfist to his head.

If this were a streetfight and your backfist didn't hurt him, it wouldn't matter because you would continue to hit him anyway: a roundhouse kick to his thigh, a punch to his ribs, a punch to his neck, and so on. Some of these blows will hurt him while others will only distract him. The idea is to continue hitting, to wear him down so that he can no longer continue.

TRAINING WITHOUT GLOVES

When I began training in karate in 1965, there were no foam-dipped, superlight, supersoft, shiny-colored, everlasting gloves with space-age Velcro. Sparring was wild, unsophisticated, and considerably more dangerous than it is today. There were lots of injuries to the hands and fingers, not to mention to the faces that were hit. I was very happy to see protective equipment come on the scene, as I was constantly jamming my fingers and applying ice to swollen knobs on the backs of my hands.

Protective equipment, however, was met with controversy. People who didn't care for it felt it created false confidence, which permitted students to attempt techniques they wouldn't try when they were not wearing them. The controversy passed and today protective equipment is

When your hands are protected with gloves, you are more willing to try different techniques.

accepted in all but a few schools. All open tournaments require protection now, although there are some traditional tournaments that disallow it.

Without protective equipment, karate wouldn't be as popular as it is today. Although it is a rough-and-tumble activity, there are fewer injuries in karate than in many other physical pursuits. This can be attributed primarily to safety equipment.

The early protestors were correct in saying protective equipment gives students greater courage and confidence to try techniques they wouldn't attempt without it. Although they meant this to be negative, it isn't. By trying something

Without gloves, you can penetrate small openings.

new, students are exposing themselves to a greater variety of concepts and techniques and developing more confidence.

As valuable as hand gear is in training, however, you won't be wearing it on the street. It is important, therefore, to practice occasionally without it. You will experience a different feel to your punches. As light as the gloves are, they still make a difference; your hands will feel lighter and less bulky without them. You will be amazed at how easily you can get punches into smaller openings since your bare fist is virtually half the size of your gloved hand.

You will notice a big difference blocking, especially if you have consistently allowed the gloves to absorb your opponent's blows. For example, catching your opponent's backfist knuckles against the tender surface of the back of your hand will definitely let you know that you have been blocking improperly.

Train without gloves from time to time. It can be a real eye-opener.

BLOCKING

Sport karate has been both beneficial and detrimental in affecting the way we block. It has been beneficial because it has forced us to evolve from the old, traditional hard blocks to faster and more efficient ways of stopping or deflecting offensive techniques. Sport karate has been detrimental because blocking is frequently ignored or executed ineffectively in the rush to get in and get a quick point before the two-minute round is over.

As a white belt, I studied a system that used traditional blocking. In fact, I spent my first three years repetitiously practicing blocks whose effectiveness I secretly questioned against someone throwing a flurry of fast, hard, close-range techniques. They worked well against other traditional karate students, who attacked from deep forward stances and took large, telegraphing lunge steps forward. But what about the streetfighter who might be bobbing, weaving, and dancing in and out of range?

The traditional inside block is executed by chambering the blocking arm . . .

One of the premises I was taught for the traditional blocks is that they can cause injury to the attacking limb. I discovered, however, that they hurt my arm, too. The advent of arm and shin guards took care of that problem, but the blocks were still slow and left me vulnerable to other attacks.

By 1970, there were many fighting styles being used in competition, which was to have a melting-pot effect on the way competitors fought, specifically on the way they blocked. Fewer people were using the traditional, stiff, robot techniques indicative of the early years. They were moving more, employing more combinations, using techniques from other

. . . and then striking the opponent's arm. Too slow!

systems, and experimenting with more effective ways to prevent getting hit.

Tournaments taught competitors that checking, deflecting, bobbing, and ducking were all effective methods of stopping attacks. It is my opinion that the various kung fu systems introduced many of these defenses, but of course that is open to conjecture. Nonetheless, by the early 1970s, tournaments had created more efficient ways to block, some of which were effective for self-defense situations as well. Today, tournament fighters continue to evaluate and experiment with ways to avoid getting hit, and students will only get better

A simple sweep block takes very little movement to deflect a punch.

in the years to come.

On the other hand, tournaments have created some sloppy and dangerous blocking techniques. Let's examine some blocking concepts that are especially poor.

Compare the range of motion of the blocking arm with the photographs on pages 50-51.

Not blocking

When a competitor doesn't block, it's sometimes done in error and sometimes deliberately as part of the tournament game. Lower belts will neglect to block because they are concentrating only on offensive fighting, forgetting that if the opponent hits first, they may not get a chance to get their technique off.

Children under eight years of age may block well in structured drills but block poorly in unstructured sparring. This is because the part of their brain that controls reflexes hasn't fully matured. Advanced adults who are not blocking well are doing so because of poor training, usually due to an overemphasis on scoring points.

Some seasoned competitors have learned there are at least three times when they can deliberately not block: when competing against a slow fighter, when sacrificing a limb to an attack, and when turning their back on an opponent.

When competing against a slow fighter, you, the seasoned veteran, will attempt to be first to the punch. Let's say you are competing against an opponent with sluggish kicks. As he slowly raises his leg in preparation to throw a roundhouse, you ignore his leg and lunge at him with a backfist, gambling that your technique is faster than his.

Sacrifice blocking occurs when you deliberately absorb your opponent's blow to a nontarget area. The most common sacrifice block is the shoulder lift, a defense used against a high roundhouse kick. As the kick speeds your way, you raise your shoulder and lean your head and body away. The foot hits your shoulder, a nontarget area, and you counter with a quick punch to your opponent's middle.

Another popular sacrifice block is when a kick is absorbed against the forearms. This is done by holding your forearms in front of you and letting the padded foot smash into them.

The third method of sacrifice blocking is one of the most glaring examples of how playing the tournament game can lead to problems on the street. Sacrificing the back is a trick that works well in those tournaments that have made the back a nontarget area. Say your opponent is moving in with a hard, fast technique that overwhelms you. Instead of trying to block it and risk getting scored on, you turn your back so the only target available is the nontarget area. You may get a warning, but the theory is that getting a warning is better than letting your opponent get a point.

What about the street?

All of these methods work in tournaments because of the way the tournament game is played. Competitors' blows are cushioned with hand and foot guards, which protect the attacker as well as the defender. Fighters can choose to not block or to use sacrifice blocks and not be concerned that their opponents will hit them full force with bare knuckles or hard-soled shoes, or stick them with a knife.

If you are not blocking because you are more concerned about your offensive techniques, you are developing a dangerous habit that must be corrected immediately. If an attacker hits you first because you didn't block, you may never get the opportunity to use your techniques.

Many karate schools emphasize offensive techniques and minimize blocking exercises. In time, the student believes that the most important elements in training are the offensive techniques and, ultimately, scoring. This is completely wrong. If this has been the type of school you have trained in, it is imperative that you accept the fact that blocking is just as important — sometimes more important — than hitting. It is not difficult to overcome this weakness but it does require some concentrated practice.

Not blocking and trying to beat your opponent to the punch could get you hurt in the street if you miscalculate the situation. It is important that you thoroughly evaluate this practice from the standpoint of its applicability in a real fight. If you are defending yourself, do you really want to take the chance of letting the attacker hit you as you try to get your blow in first? You can get a point for this in competition because the first technique to score gets the point. In a real fight, however, your hit may not hurt the attacker but his unblocked technique may hurt you. Beating the attacker to the punch is what streetfighting is all about. But give his attack the respect it deserves and block or evade it.

Absorbing a roundhouse kick with your shoulder works in competition, but are you willing to risk it against hard street shoes?

Absorbing a side kick from a streetfighter wearing street shoes may injure or momentarily paralyze your arms.

Work on blocking and countering drills that will imprint the significance of blocking in your mind. Design drills where your opponent actually makes controlled contact with you if you fail to block. This contact can be with or without safety equipment and as light or as hard as you and your partner agree to. You will be surprised at how quickly your defensive fighting will improve.

Blocking a head-high roundhouse kick with your shoulder works in tournaments because the impact is controlled and the kicker is wearing foot guards. Is this a block you want to use in the street, where an assailant wearing hard-soled shoes really wants to take your head off? If the answer is no, then you may want to consider another defense.

If you like to block side kicks by absorbing the impact with your forearms, try this experiment. Have your training partner put on a pair of heavy boots and then side kick you as if he wanted to smash your navel against your spine. Cover your upper body with your forearms and let his kick smash into them. After your arms heal, try it again when he is wearing running shoes. Feels a little better, but not much. In the real world, absorbing straight-in, powerful kicks with your bare arms will result in injuries ranging from short-term paralysis to broken bones.

Turning your back on an opponent in a real fight is suicide. If you do this in tournaments, it will develop into a habit faster than any other practice. How you train is how you will react in a real fight. Imagine this: the street punk advances toward you, pulls a knife, and you assume your stance. He lunges, slashes the air with the blade, and you react as you have in practice and in competition — you turn your back.

A knife feels like ice when it penetrates your kidney.

Sport karate has few techniques to defend against

Think back to the last tournament you attended and make a list of all the hand techniques you saw. Your list will look something like this:
• Reverse punch

Turning your back on a fast streetfighter may be the last move you ever make.

- Straight punch
- Backfist
- Chop
- Ridgehand

These five techniques are the most common methods of attacking with the hands in sport karate. As a result, fighting styles oriented toward competition direct the majority of their defensive training only against these techniques. Martial artists should never limit themselves to such a narrow field of techniques and angles of attack.

If you are a colored belt or above, you have probably noticed that white belts can be difficult to spar. In fact, most black belts will admit that the most unorthodox sparring opponent is the white belt. One reason for this is that the beginner's techniques are not as clean and polished nor are they executed in nice, straight lines and perfectly formed arcs, as with the advanced students. Their actions and reactions are unpredictable, which can throw off a more experienced student who has been conditioned to expect karate techniques executed in a certain manner.

I teach the boxer's jab in my school. It's a wonderful tool that can be used to harass, keep an aggressive opponent away, and set up a second attack. Most karate students never practice the jab and, as a result, are easy to hit with it. I've even had opponents ignore my jabs because they felt they were not real karate techniques. Usually a couple of solid smacks to the forehead convinces them of the jab's validity.

In a street confrontation you can be attacked with anything. You may be attacked with something similar to the listed tournament techniques, but you will more likely have to defend against wild roundhouse punches, shoves, grabs, short jabs, flailing arms, eye gouges, and clinches. Some of these may be executed along the same paths as the five tournament techniques, but some will be in patterns you are not used to, making your standard blocks ineffective against them.

To remedy this, you need to work on blocking drills that improve your ability to defend against a wide range of attacks from different angles. Experiment beyond the standard karate movements; how would you defend yourself against a trained boxer or the unorthodox movements of an untrained person flailing his arms at you like a madman?

To be safe, expect anything in the street. When a student says, "You would never see that in a real fight," I immediately counter with, "How do you know?" There are excellent streetfighters with well-honed fighting skills, even martial-art experience, and there are others who will attack with wild and crazy techniques.

Examine techniques from all angles. For example, let's take a look at a common fighting technique that is often successful against well-trained karate students.

The common tackle

A tackle is executed by wrapping the arms around the victim's waist, ramming with the shoulder, and either pushing the victim into a wall or picking him up and dropping him onto his back. To examine it, let's break the tackle down into several stages: the initial stance, the takeoff, the moment the arms start to encircle the waist, the clinch, the push backwards, and the takedown. You might react at the beginning of the attack, or maybe you won't see him until he grabs you. Since you don't know at what point you will see your attacker and realize what is happening, it is important that you train to respond at each stage.

STAGE I. The initial stance for the tackle is assumed by crouching slightly, the legs spread and the arms held out like a wrestler. This posture is held for only a second, perhaps longer if the attacker is drunk or a stalking wrestler. Defensively, you do not have enough time to assume your sparring stance so you must react quickly and decisively. Lunging in and jamming his closest arm against his chest and then slamming a bottom fist down onto his shoulder muscles is one option that uses the element of surprise and puts the attacker on the defensive.

STAGE II. He lunges toward you. How you react to his takeoff depends on how far away he is. If he is within kicking range, you can sidestep and drive a kick into his lead leg or his stomach. If he is within arms' reach, you can sidestep, push his closest arm into his chest, and strike him hard in the face with your palm.

STAGE III. There are several possible responses as his arms start to encircle your waist. It depends on what feels right, based on your body position and your attacker's body position. You can sidestep and push his arms away as just mentioned. You can also push his arms down and then rake his face with your fingers. You can shuffle backwards, grab his hair, and pull him to the ground.

STAGE IV. Once his arms are around you and he is driving you into a wall, you should be hitting him with everything

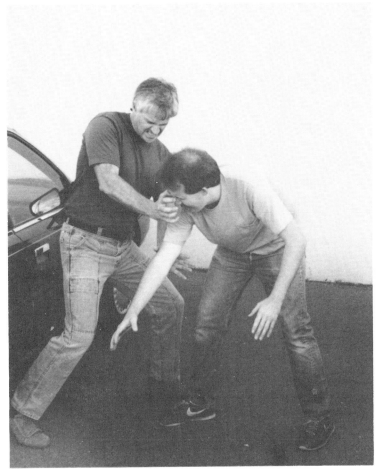

A streetfighter may not know any tournament techniques and attack with unorthodox moves such as the common tackle. Jam his tackling arm and claw his face.

you have. Direct your hand techniques to the closest targets, such as his ears, eyes, cheeks, neck, and the top of his head. Your objective is to weaken him so that you can escape his clinch.

STAGE V. If he has dropped you on your back, you need to react quickly while his arms are still wrapped around your waist. Again, strike the vulnerable targets of his face and head.

* * * * *

As you can see, defending against a street attack is more complex than a tournament backfist. It is important, therefore, to broaden your defense repertoire to include street situations. You need to scrutinize all possible angles, distances, and the variety of things the arms, fists, and legs can do.

To reiterate, never rule out anything a streetfighter will try. Not all of them are polished technicians. Some are mental cases with extraordinary strength, some are drunk and thinking with brains pickled with alcohol, and others are narcotic users, desperate for their next fix.

Anything is possible. Plan for it.

3 Kicking

KICKING THE HEAD

When executed with great speed and flexibility, head kicks are thrilling to see and even more fun to do. There is something very satisfying about smacking an opponent behind his ear with a perfectly timed roundhouse kick. It dramatically displays the fighter's skills, it thrills audiences, and it inspires judges to award points to the fighter with the highest foot.

Some tournaments even award two points for head kicks. The idea is to make competitors kick more, which keeps spectator interest up, since match after match of reverse punches gets pretty boring to watch.

I won't get into the argument about whether the two-point rule is fair to fighters who study a style that emphasizes hand techniques. I won't even complain that one of my students lost after she scored with a backfist to the groin, a powerful punch to the face, and another to the floating rib. She lost because her opponent earned four points with two pop-up kicks to her head.

I won't complain because I don't care, other than I hate to see a student lose a match because of a rule that makes tournament fighting unrealistic. (I'll put my money on a throat punch over a flip kick to the head anytime.) The real concern should be whether or not head kicks are a viable technique in a street confrontation.

Kicking to the head in a real fight can be difficult for many reasons, including:

- Street clothes may be too tight.
- Some shoes and boots are too heavy.
- You lose power when you kick higher than your waist.
- The head is a mobile target and is easy to miss.
- Maintaining your balance on one leg can be precarious, especially on wet grass, pavement, or loose gravel.
- A good streetfighter can grab your foot.
- Head kicks are relatively easy to block.
- A streetfighter probably expects you to try for his head.
- You won't have time to stretch out.
- A blow to the head has an unreliable effect.
- It takes more time to kick to the head.
- It takes time to return your foot to the ground.
- High kicks leave the groin and support leg open to a counterattack.
- High kicks are usually telegraphed.

A valuable lesson

One time, a second degree black belt in a Korean kicking art joined my school to improve his hand techniques. He had amazing flexibility and could execute beautiful high kicks. He asked to spar with my students his first day in class. I wasn't sure if he wanted to test himself to see where he fit into my school or if he wanted to convince me of his expertise. In either case, I decided I would show him what a streetfighting art was all about.

I picked one of my green belts, a young woman with two years of training. They bowed and began to circle one another. The black belt fired a high, arcing hook kick to her head. She evaded the kick and hit him with a roundhouse kick to his support leg. The black belt then executed a nose-high side kick, which was met with a block and a counter front kick to his groin. The black belt made one final effort at high kicking with a fast-as-a-speeding-bullet roundhouse. Although it partially hit her cheek, she blocked most of it and was still able to slam a punch into his thigh and land another groin kick.

The experienced black belt, whose basics were in head kicks, had his hands full when he tried to fight a less-skilled fighter, whose roots were in kicking and punching the legs. It didn't take long, however, before the black belt started directing his kicks to lower targets.

This match was good for both fighters. The black belt was

A high roundhouse kick is fun to do and looks pretty, but is it too risky for the street?

made to see that a repertoire of all head kicks could get him in trouble. The green belt, who was not always convinced of the risk of high kicking, actually convinced herself by reacting as she had been taught. She now teaches beginners about the danger of head-hunting.

There are some karate students who may be able to kick effectively to the head in a streetfight, regardless of the negative elements listed above. If you possess such exceptional speed, power, and flexibility that you can overcome all of the drawbacks, then have at it. If you are not so blessed, then you had better consider lower targets.

A high kick is vulnerable to an easy block and counter.

High kicks against a boxer

The controversy over who is superior, a karate fighter or a boxer, has gone on for years. There have been numerous experiments with a variety of outcomes. I saw one where the issue of kicking to the head was significant.

The experiment was conducted by a former International Karate Association world champion. He attempted three basic head kicks against a champion Golden Gloves boxer who was a representative for the east coast in AAU competition. All blows on both sides were full-powered, full-contact hits.

The boxer kept his hands high, effectively covering his head.

A slow back kick is easy to block and counter.

A rear-leg roundhouse couldn't land but a lead-leg kick glanced off the boxer's head. All of the high roundhouse kicks were easily picked off and the boxer would counter by rushing inside and landing hard blows to the karate man's ribs. The karate man was successful, however, with offensive and defensive roundhouses to the inner and outer thighs. The boxer later complained that the low blows felt like knives stabbing his legs.

The karate man didn't attempt the front kick to the boxer's head, probably because of the high guard. Front kicks to the middle proved effective whenever the boxer advanced. The karate man then attempted a front jump kick and the boxer quickly covered, moved in, and countered with a solid right to his forehead. The karate man was hit so hard that he didn't attempt the technique again.

The boxer always saw the side kick coming. He would sidestep, push the karate man off balance, and punch him hard in the back.

The karate man threw two spinning back kicks and the boxer stepped back out of range. When the karate man made a third attempt, the boxer ducked under it and hooked a punch into his opponent's kidneys.

The karate man found that leg sweeps worked especially well, as did knee strikes. When the boxer was rooted in a solid stance, the sweeps wouldn't budge him. But when the boxer was driven back, the lead leg was swept easily and he went down. A knee technique was effective, although executed accidentally, after the boxer ducked a reverse punch. When the boxer's head went down, the karate man's leg lifted for a front kick and he accidentally smashed the boxer's nose.

This informal and less than scientific study is not the final answer as to which fighting system is better. It is food for thought, though, when considering low kicks or high kicks.

KICKING LOW

Kicking at an opponent's legs is not allowed in point karate tournaments; in fact, you can get a warning for even faking at the legs. One of the reasons for this rule is that leg kicking is so easy to do and so hard to defend against, competitors would be doing it all the time. Spectators would then lose interest since leg kicking is not very interesting to watch.

Secondly, it's dangerous to kick to the limbs since an uncontrolled blow to a joint could be crippling. Even medium-strength impact to a leg muscle could drop a tournament fighter and cause enough pain and/or injury to prevent him from continuing.

If a kick to the leg is easy to do and hard to block and contact is potentially debilitating, then doesn't it make sense that it may be a viable technique for self-defense?

It's fun to kick high! It's a beautiful sight to see a roundhouse kick lift, arc through the air with blinding speed, and stop a hair-width away from an opponent's earlobe. The opponent feels vulnerable and the kicker feels great. As "Super Foot" Bill Wallace says, "Anyone can kick low, but I like to kick high because it makes me feel good."

We have all seen the Bruce Lee movies and been awed by his incredible kicking prowess. Few can match his awesome speed, power, and accuracy. His cinematic kicks were beauty in motion and the epitome of high kicking.

But did you know Bruce Lee didn't believe in high kicks when involved in a real altercation? Indeed, this master of high kicks on the screen said he would never use them for self-defense. For that he preferred to kick low.

It's true that leg kicks are not flashy, nor are they visually impressive. But in a street encounter, does flash matter? The bottom line is not how high your kicks are but whether or not you survive to walk away from the fight.

WHY ARE LEG ATTACKS EFFECTIVE?

There are several reasons leg attacks are effective in the street:
- Leg attacks are painful.
- There is usually less clothing worn on the legs.
- Legs are easier to hit than upper-body targets.

• Leg attacks will weaken an opponent's foundation.
• Leg attacks set up an opponent for a takedown.
• Most opponents expect attacks to the head.

Leg attacks are painful

The bottom line in a self-defense situation is to prevent an attacker from hurting you. Since you don't always have the opportunity to run away, the next step is to use enough force to stop the aggression. The legs are a good target because they are so vulnerable — you can easily stun an attacker with a minor kick and thus give him pause to rethink what he

Leg kicks hurt.

is doing. You can also hit them hard enough to break bones, if the situation is serious and warrants extreme force.

Hitting the leg hurts. If you are sitting in a chair reading this, relax your right thigh and, without too much force, punch your upper leg. Hurts, doesn't it? In fact, it sends a minor shock wave from your hip to your knee. Can you imagine getting struck there with the hard sole of a shoe?

Next, take that coffee cup you just drained and lightly tap yourself on your kneecap and again farther down on your shin. Smarts, huh? How would the hard edge of a shoe feel slamming into those same targets? It also hurts to jam your thumb into the center of your calf and the inside of your thigh. Imagine a well-placed kick, traveling at fifty to seventy miles per hour, smashing into the same, soft tissue.

There is less clothing on the legs

Usually, the lower part of the body is not covered with clothing as thick and heavy as the upper body. This is important when you consider the countless stories of assaults where a bullet did not penetrate the victim's heavy winter coat or a knife failed to slice through a thick shirt.

A cold winter day will find people wearing hats, scarves, gloves, and bulky coats, but their legs will only be covered with blue jeans or slacks. This light covering makes the legs a more vulnerable target for your well-placed, powerful kicks.

Legs are easier to hit

Another consideration on a cold day is how well stretched you are. Cold weather has a tendency to stiffen the muscles, constricting your flexibility and preventing you from kicking high. Kicks to an opponent's knee or thigh muscles, however, are easily within the range of your flexibility, even on the coldest days.

Weakening an opponent's foundation

Your legs are your support base, giving strength to your techniques and providing mobility to move in and out of range and the ability to duck and weave. When your muscles and/or nerve endings have been impacted, your strength and mobility are drastically diminished. Additionally, the physical shock will weaken and alter your mental facilities.

Let's say you are confronted by someone who, by his actions and statements, convinces you he is about to throw a punch. Instead of waiting for his attack, you hook a powerful heel strike into the side of his thigh. He tries to hide the pain, but his face is starting to knot. He throws a wild punch, but you are faster with a kick into his shin, followed by a

Soften the attacker's leg with a hook kick . . .

roundhouse kick to the other side of his thigh.

There are two things that may happen at this point. One possibility is that the assailant's legs will buckle from the blows and he will be left writhing on the ground. The other is that your blows haven't been accurate or hard enough to make him fall, but you have at least caught his attention by hurting his leg. He is now thinking about himself rather than you. He is not sure what you are going to do to him next. Once he is psyched-out and hurt, it won't be long before he loses his ability and desire to continue.

. . . and take him down.

Takedowns

One of the most psychologically disconcerting techniques you can do to an attacker is to take his feet out from under him and let him crash unceremoniously to the earth. Psychologically he feels vulnerable, and physically he is vulnerable to a follow-up attack. It requires precise timing to unbalance a fighter and then follow through with a takedown.

One takedown that works well in the street requires that you first "soften" an attacker's legs before you execute the move. This softening process involves smashing your kicks into the sensitive area of one or both of his legs. Even if the blows don't knock him to the floor, his thoughts will be directed toward the pain, making it much easier to take him down with a simple push or sweep.

Hitting low when he thinks high

If you ask the average untrained person to assume a fighting stance, he usually assumes something that looks like a boxer: feet staggered and hands held high. This is a natural position based on mimicry and an expectation that an attack will be to his upper body and head.

This is exactly what you want him to think. His hands are high and his thinking is divided between protecting his head and how he is going to attack you. Kicking him in the legs at this point is as easy as a walk in the park. You can even set him up by executing a fake to his head to ensure his attention stays high before slamming a hard kick into his knee.

Another variation is to get him to attack your head. To hit high he must think high, and it is at that exact moment that you counter low. This can be accomplished by beating him to the punch or by executing a simultaneous block and counter. No matter how skilled he is, it will take a moment for him to mentally shift gears so he can defend his exposed lower half.

The fighting principle involved here is called high/low, which is partly based on another principle called action/

reaction. The action/reaction principle states that action is faster than reaction. A fighter's eyes must see the attack and send an image to the brain. The brain must translate the image as a threat and then send a command to the muscles to block or evade. This process will take too long and reaction will be too late if the low attack is swift and sure.

Timing

Hitting the legs of an attacker as he moves toward you takes speed and timing. One method is to strike as he is moving but before he launches his actual attack. This is easy against a fighter who moves his body before he initiates his kick or punch. If your opponent does lead with his attacking limb, you have to be faster to hit him first, be able to sidestep

If he punches high, jam his punch and kick him low.

his charge, or step into him and interrupt his move.

Another easy way to strike the legs is during the process of blocking a kick. Although blocks are normally used to stop or deflect, they can also be used to inflict pain on an attacker's leg. Say you are defending against a hard front kick. Instead of deflecting the leg to the side, use the opportunity to slam your fist or forearm into the side of his calf. To add more pain, you can follow with your other fist into the soft tissues of his inner thigh or into the extremely vulnerable kneecap. Since both of your hands are involved with the counter, you must be fast, be aware of the attacker's hands, and you must get back out of range quickly. Another approach is to sidestep

Catch the attacker's leg and punish it.

his kick and drive your knee into the side or back of his
thigh.

Targets

Recommended targets on an opponent's leg are the ankle
bone, top of the foot, Achilles tendon, calf, shin, knee, inner
thigh, outer thigh, and back of thigh. Actually, just about any
area that is struck is vulnerable to pain, although these targets
are particularly vulnerable. (Targets will be discussed in
greater detail in Chapter 6.)

Of course, the degree of pain or injury is dependent on
the amount of force behind the blow as well as the
vulnerability of the target struck. For example, you could kick
someone in the front of the thigh, an area that is relatively
tolerant to pain, and get little or no response from the assailant.
But if you were to kick someone with the same force in the
knee, an extremely vulnerable target, the result would be
considerably more painful and injurious.

Attacking the legs is often neglected in tournament-oriented
systems because the emphasis is on targets that earn points.
This is unfortunate because the legs are one of the best targets
to hit in a self-defense situation. Attacking the legs is similar
to cutting down a tree with an ax. Rather than hacking at
the leaves and branches, you would be wiser to chop at the
trunk, weaken the support base, and bring the tree down
more efficiently and quickly.

Leg attacks may not be as fancy as Bruce Lee's high hook
kicks, but they work. And in the street, where things can
get pretty ugly, that's all that really matters.

KICKING WITH STREET SHOES

The custom of training barefoot was established when
American servicemen returned home from the Orient and
introduced the martial arts to America. Today there are a
few karate schools that train in running shoes, but most follow
the old custom. Additionally, training and competing barefoot
is safer on the opponent and makes wearing padded foot

gear easier. Particularly important is the wearing of foot gear, since insurance companies are asking for greater protection for the competitor.

This is a good requirement for sport, but what about the street? When was the last time you had to defend yourself while barefoot? We are a society that wears shoes, so there is a much greater chance we will have a confrontation while our feet are covered.

Do you need to adjust your foot position when kicking the bag with street shoes?

Just as it is important to occasionally train without hand gear, it is also important to train from time to time while wearing different types of street shoes. Put on your running shoes and practice all your kicks against low and high targets. The first thing you will notice is that there is additional weight felt in your hips and knees. Although modern running shoes are light, you will notice that they still slow your kicks a little.

Now experiment with kicking the bags and see if your running shoes make a difference. Your foot positions may be different than when you are barefoot. You might kick harder because of the extra protection. If your shoes are loose, one may fly off. If you have slick soles, you might slip and slide on the floor and create an unstable support leg. If your soles grip the floor too well, it may prevent your stationary foot from rotating.

Now try your dress shoes or boots. The biggest difference you will notice is they are heavier than the running shoes and definitely heavier than bare feet. There will be a decrease in speed and perhaps some pain in the knee joint when you snap the leg back from the kick. When you kick with the ball of the foot, it will be difficult to curl the toes, which will affect the front kick and the roundhouse.

Many years ago I kicked a man with a roundhouse and injured my foot. I was wearing Vietnam jungle boots, and it was impossible to curl my toes back to make impact with the ball of my foot. I hadn't given this any thought before the fight, but I sure thought about it as I was limping around afterward. Months later I was kicking a heavy bag while wearing street shoes and did it again. I'm a slow learner, but it didn't take a third time for me to figure out that you can pull the toes back while barefoot but you can't while wearing heavy shoes.

Pulling the toes back is less of a problem with the front kick because even if your shoes were unbendable, you could still flex your foot upward enough to strike with the bottom of the shoe. Of course, you can always kick with the toe if you are wearing heavy, steel-toed boots.

Another consideration is blocking. Swatting at the feet, as is often seen in competition, will injure your fingers if you try it against an attacker wearing a hard shoe. In the street, you won't have the protection of padded hand gear, and the attacker won't be wearing padded foot gear. If you are a swatter or you like to sacrifice your shoulder or upper arm to kicks, you should rethink whether this habit is in your best interest. Even a weak kick that probably wouldn't hurt if it hit your body could cause debilitating injury were it to hit your hand or some other vulnerable area.

STREET CLOTHES

Your kicks will also feel different when you are wearing street clothes. One of the first streetfights I had after I began studying karate revealed the difference between *gi* (karate uniform) pants and cord trousers. A drunk had jumped me outside a fast-food joint and I defended myself with a beautifully placed crescent kick to his throat. As I stood over his prone body, I could feel a distinctive cool breeze. I looked down and discovered the entire crotch of my pants blowing in the wind. (Some pants are so tight that they can even prohibit *low* kicks.)

It's a good idea to work out in your street clothes to see what you can and cannot do. Check to see if you can kick while wearing tight jeans, dress slacks, a tight skirt, a long coat, or high-heeled shoes.

There is no need to get fanatical about this and wear your *gi* pants in public, as I have seen some people do. But if you take the time, you can find clothes, especially pants, that make the fashion statement you want while allowing you to move and kick.

STRIKING WITH THE KNEES

In the many tournaments I have attended, only once have I seen a point awarded for a knee strike. Knee strikes are effective weapons, but they are rarely considered by karate students, and never by competitors. Rare is the judge who would award points for such attacks anyway. Nonetheless, knee techniques are effective and powerful weapons for the street, especially when the fight gets in close.

There are two directions of force in which the knees can be used: upward and roundhouse. Because the knees are close to the body, they are sturdy, powerful, and able to forcefully penetrate defenses. They are excellent for close-range fighting.

Upward knee strike

When you are in a clinch and trying to get a position of advantage, knee strikes work well because you can pull the attacker even closer and pummel away. You can execute the upward knee strike with relatively good balance because it doesn't require the same amount of body lean that other kicks do. A side kick, for example, would be impossible to execute because of the necessary body English and leg lift. On the other hand, if you are able to take only one step while in a clinch, then you can execute an upward knee strike.

Knee strikes work well when you can pull the attacker into your striking range. For example, you block the attacker's punch, step in, grab behind his neck, and pull him forward into your upward knee strike. The impact is virtually doubled because the head and knee are moving into one another.

Another way to generate power with the knee strike is to use it as a surprise technique, such as when an attacker grabs you and pulls you toward him. Instead of bumping chests, move forward and drive your knee into his groin or upper thigh.

Roundhouse knee strike

The roundhouse knee is used the same as the upward knee strike, although it does require that you lean your body away slightly (though not to the extent necessary for delivering a roundhouse kick). Its power comes from the thrust of the knee as well as the rotation of the hips.

The roundhouse knee works particularly well in two types

An upward knee strike can be delivered with good balance and power.

A roundhouse knee strike is often an unexpected counter.

of close-fighting situations. Say you are in a clinch and the attacker is trying to hit you with his knees as he pulls and pushes you. You have tried to hit him a couple of times with upward knee strikes, only to clash your kneecap with his attempted knee strikes. You need to change your angle of attack. At a moment when you are in a stable position, lean your body to one side just enough to execute a roundhouse knee strike that will go over and around his upraised knee and into his ribs.

The second situation finds you too close to kick. For example, an attacker has moved in close in an attempt to wrestle you. Knock his arms to the side and grab one of his upper arms with both of your hands. Lean slightly in the same direction and roundhouse knee him in the abdomen or ribs.

KICKING WITH THE SHIN
Although the shins are deadly weapons, they are rarely used by karate students. A Thai kickboxer, however, uses shin kicks to kick full force into the face of his opponent. There are stories of Thai kickboxers striking their shins with hammers and repetitiously kicking tree trunks to toughen the striking surface. This is potentially damaging to the skin, bones, and nerves, and it's also unnecessary, since the technique is effective without extra conditioning.

Striking with the shin is a medium-range technique. If the attacker is at a greater distance, you should kick with your foot, and if he is very close, you should use your knees. Shin strikes fill that in-between range.

Good targets to strike are the groin, upper thighs, lower ribs, and kidneys. The shin kick is executed like an upward front snap kick, or in a circular fashion, like a roundhouse kick. It is powerful and can be delivered with surprise because it appears you are too close to kick effectively.

KICKING WITH THE THIGH
Striking with the thigh is done at even closer ranges than

Kicking with the shin bone can be devastating.

with the knee. It is not as strong as knee and shin kicks because it has a shorter distance to travel. Nonetheless, it is effective when the assailant is virtually on top of you — say pressing you against a wall and pinning your arms. Use upward and roundhouse thigh strikes to force the assailant back.

KICKING WHEN THE ASSAILANT IS DOWN

Some tournaments allow contestants two or three seconds to score on an opponent when he is on the floor; some do not. Those that do allow it do so with restrictions because of the potential for injury. Punches and kicks to the head are especially dangerous when the head is supported by the floor. Body strikes are safer, and many tournaments allow them.

Despite the rules, many competitors never attempt to hit a downed opponent. They either consider it unsportsmanlike or have never been taught the technique.

Sportsmanship doesn't count on the street; you are not getting a trophy for being a nice guy. Your concern is to survive the confrontation and escape. Kicking the attacker when he is down is an opportune time to get the upper hand.

Actually, you don't have to wait until the attacker is all the way down to finish him off. If he starts to fall as a result of your blow or foot sweep, follow up immediately with hard kicks before he hits the ground. His mind is on the ground rushing toward him, making him vulnerable to your attacks. Take advantage of his mental focus by continuing to hit him as he falls and after he lands, and don't stop until he says he has had enough (but be wary after you let up) or he can no longer fight.

Hit him anywhere it will benefit you. If he is just starting to fall, then work on his already unstable legs by kicking his thighs, knees, and ankles. If he is down, work on his ribs, groin, and abdomen with the idea of making him curl into a ball. If he starts to push himself up with his arms, weaken his support by kicking his elbows and wrist joints. If the assailant is armed, you should kick his head. A kick anywhere in the face will stun him and cause his eyes to water profusely so that he cannot see and thus cannot press the attack.

Develop some drills to get you to think about continuing to fight after your assailant falls. He is in a weak position and you should take advantage of it.

KICKING THE ASSAILANT WHEN YOU ARE DOWN

When you fall to the floor in competition, most rules allow you to attempt to score within two or three seconds. Some competitors do, but most just lie helplessly waiting for the referee to move in and stop the action. They don't know what to do because they are used to fighting on two feet. When they fall, their minds tell them the fight is over.

In reality, a street assailant will take full advantage of your position. He will continue to kick, punch, or perhaps jump on you. If you have trained to stop fighting when you are

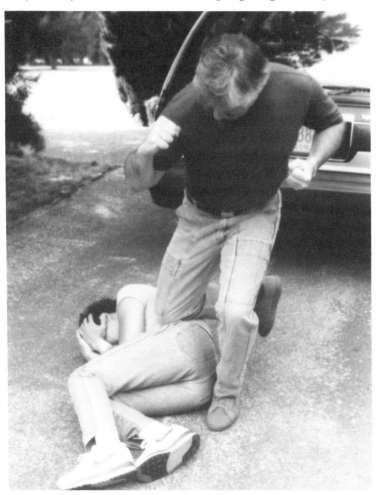

Finish him off with a knee drop to the ribs.

down, you are in trouble.

Use your kicks to keep the attacker away. Your kicks will keep him on the defensive while you work yourself into a position to get up. Kick fast and furiously and *keep kicking* until you are all the way up. Kick anything you can hit; remember, you want to keep him busy. If you are provided with a clear choice, however, aim for such vulnerable targets as the protruding ankle bone, shin, knee joint, front and rear thigh muscles, and the groin.

* * * * *

The legs are the most powerful weapons you have. Some tournament kicks are okay, but in the street, where there are no rules, there are many more kicking techniques and targets open to you. Before you can use them, you must open your mind to their existence and practice them.

You never know what can happen in a real fight, so never exclude anything from your training.

4 Close-Range Techniques

Bruce Lee and a famous judo champion were once working out at Bruce's house. The judoka (a practitioner of judo) had trained a little in karate but couldn't begin to match Bruce's extraordinary speed. Every time the judoka would set himself to attack, Bruce would reach out and tap his head with a finger.

Noticing that Bruce's techniques were all long-range movements, the judoka asked what he would do if they both started their fight on the ground, a position where the judoka was highly proficient. Bruce looked at him for a moment and then replied, "I would just walk away."

Bruce knew he could not compete in close and on the ground because it was not his area of expertise. He was smart enough to not jump into an arena where he was clearly at a disadvantage. Later, Bruce perfected his close-range fighting techniques by working with top wrestlers and jujutsu experts.

Most karate students are ineffective at close-range fighting. Tournament fighters train to move around and hit targets from the most remote position possible. Many streetfighters, however, prefer to get inside the punching and kicking ranges and wrestle. Once this happens, the average karate student is out of his element.

This is unfortunate because karate does have many weapons that are effective at close range. Tournament-oriented students seldom practice them, however, because their training emphasis is on flamboyant tournament techniques.

To survive a streetfight, it is important that you train on techniques that can be used when you are nose-to-nose with the attacker. When he is within kissing range, your hook kick, high roundhouse kick, and diving backfists are worthless. Let's take a look at some of the things you can do, especially from a common position called "the clinch."

THE CLINCH

Real fights often begin with a chest-bumping ritual, with the combatants nose-to-nose and threatening each other. They are too close to throw long-range techniques so they begin with a push, followed by a roundhouse punch, then maybe a sloppy kick and, inevitably, a clinch.

Clinching, as is done in boxing, occurs when you are holding the attacker's upper arms and he is holding yours. You are both trying to prevent the other from attacking as you shuffle around, maneuvering for the most advantageous position. It is a position that is in between hitting and grappling.

Clinching is usually thought of in relation to boxing, where two tired fighters hang on to each other and stall until being saved by the bell. In a streetfight, it is not a time to rest or get careless. You are still fighting, constantly looking to take advantage of any opening the attacker gives you.

Let's examine a few karate techniques that work well at close range.

Biting

Biting has a negative connotation that makes it difficult for some karate students to include it in their repertoire. It is often perceived as fighting like a baby or, even more absurd, fighting unfairly. When a situation has become physical, you should do whatever it takes to stop an attacker's aggression. There are no such things as fair techniques, only techniques that get the job done.

Biting will definitely get the job done. It is not only excruciatingly painful, it also carries an element of surprise. Say an attacker is holding you in a bear hug from the front, your arms are pinned, and your feet are dangling in the air. Your flailing kicks to his shins have not affected him and you can feel yourself growing weaker from his crushing grip.

This is an excellent opportunity to bite. You are close to the targets, you don't have to assume a stance, and you don't need great power or speed. Move in like Count Dracula and take a chomp out of his neck, ear, cheek, or nose. You will

If your arms are pinned, take a bite out of him.

feel him loosen his grip enough for you to make your escape.

Another example finds you in a clinch, struggling hard to hold the arms of a much larger person. Although you are barely holding his upper arms back, he is able to stretch his open palm toward your face, probably with the intention of pushing your head back. Don't miss the opportunity to take a chomp out of the first finger that gets close to your mouth.

There are three methods of biting, all very painful and very effective. The first method is the basic straight bite, where you simply chomp down on the target as if you were biting into a tuna sandwich. The bunny-shake bite is the second method, which is done in the same manner that a dog attacks a rabbit. It begins with a straight chomp but instead of releasing the bite, you shake your head vigorously to increase damage to the skin. The last method is the typewriter bite. Say you are on the ground and an attacker has your upper body pinned between his legs. Execute a straight chomp to his calf and then move your head in either direction, chomping as you go.

It should be noted that although biting is an excellent streetfighting technique, there is the consideration of the AIDS virus. Biting an infected person and drawing blood could expose you to the disease.

Needless to say, you must simulate biting in class. Simulating a bite in competition will not get you a point and a real bite will get you disqualified.

Head butting

You have probably bumped heads with someone at least once in your life and know that it hurts. In fact, the pain can be excruciating and sometimes debilitating. When head butting is done purposely and directed at a vulnerable target, the technique can be most effective.

There are martial artists who specialize in breaking blocks of ice and stacks of bricks with their foreheads. If you want to do this, that's fine, but you can be proficient with the technique without performing such dramatic displays. There is no conditioning required and you do not have to develop callouses on your forehead.

Head butting is an excellent technique to use when your arms are pinned. If you are held from the front, thrust your forehead forward and strike the assailant on the nose. If you are being held from behind, drive your heel into his shins so he will lean forward, then snap your head back into his face. The pain, coupled with watering eyes, will cause sufficient distraction to enable you to execute follow-up techniques or escape.

You can also head butt when your arms are free. Say you are in a clinch and trying to grapple your attacker to the ground. Your grappling technique will be more effective if you butt him in the face to weaken him, then execute your takedown. If you are in a clinch and the attacker is starting to get you in a hold, smack your forehead into his face and make your escape.

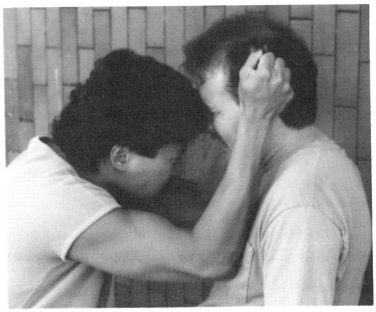

Work your arms out of the clinch, grab his ears or hair, and pull him into a head butt.

Head butting is a painful offensive and defensive technique that won't get you a tournament point (in fact, it will get you into a lot of trouble), but it will most assuredly get an attacker's attention.

Hip striking

If you have ever had a judo or jujutsu fighter execute a hip throw against you, you know that a hip thrust into your midsection can be painful. Most people are more concerned about crashing to the floor, but they are surprised when they feel the pain of a hip thrust into their pelvic area.

Although the hip strike can be used effectively without the throw, it is not a technique that you should use deliberately as an initial attack. It is effective when you need to create a distraction, gain a moment of time, create distance, or set up an attacker so you can hit him again.

Let's say you are positioned sideways in a clinch and the attacker has his arm around you, struggling to take you down. One of your arms is pinned against him and the other is on his opposite side, pulling ineffectively at his arm. Your hip is touching, or nearly touching, his body. At this point, about the only thing you can do is a hip strike.

Draw your hips away slightly and then, like an enraged hula dancer, thrust your hip into his groin/pelvic area. It is possible he will drop from the pain or, at the very least, be distracted long enough for you to get into a stronger position to defend yourself.

Shoulder thrust

You may not be football linebacker material, but the shoulder thrust can work for you. It has the element of surprise that the hip strike has, combined with even greater body momentum. It is also a versatile movement that can be used at close range or charging from a distance.

When you are clinching with an attacker, arms entwined and leaning against one another, you are in a prime position to execute a shoulder thrust. A sudden twist of the waist and thrust with your legs and you can easily drive your shoulder into his chest. Power is achieved by dropping low, bending forward at the waist, and charging like a football player. You can use this technique to either shove an attacker aside or slam into his stomach, ribs, or face to cause injury.

There are two painful variations to the shoulder thrust that can be executed from a clinch. The instant you have a free hand, encircle it around the attacker's head, pull him forward, and simultaneously smash your shoulder into his face. The second variation is to duck just enough so your shoulder is under his head and then drive your legs upward as hard as you can. If his tongue is hanging out when your shoulder smashes into his chin, he won't be able to utter a word of complaint.

As a long-range technique, the shoulder thrust can be used like a battering ram. Say an assailant is blocking your path. If he is momentarily distracted or turns away from you for whatever reason, smash your shoulder into him like a bowling ball picking off a spare.

The shoulder thrust is a surprisingly strong technique and is applicable in a number of situations. Experiment to learn what you can do with it.

Forearm strikes

Professional wrestlers like to slam each other in the upper chest with a technique they call the "forearm smash." The victim is struck on the chest just below the collar bone with the full length of the forearm. It is usually accompanied by a foot stomp on the mat to give the technique a little audio effect. The victim reacts by showering the air with saliva and then staggering around like a drunken chicken until he is struck again and finally falls.

Although it is debatable whether getting struck there will cause that dramatic of a reaction, the forearm strike is still a good technique. At close range, the forearm can be used to push an attacker away, strike upward against the jaw, push an attacker's head aside, strike the groin, block an attacker from punching or grappling, or jam the attacker's on-guard stance.

Elbow strike

An elbow strike is capable of tremendous force because it is close to the upper body and is delivered with a sharp twist of the waist, thus increasing its power. When the fight gets in close, elbow strikes can be delivered in rapid-fire succession, knocking aside everything in their path. There are four basic angles of attack: straight, upward, round, and downward.

Although most students practice elbow strikes with a clenched fist, studies show that an open hand allows for greater power and speed while the elbow is traveling toward the target. This is because a clenched fist has the tendency to make the arm tense, thus slowing down the movement. On impact, however, you can either keep your hand open or make a fist an instant before contact is made with the target. Experiment both ways to see which you like.

You don't have to wait for an opening to use an elbow strike because with a sharp, pointed elbow, you can make your own path. Anywhere you hit is going to hurt. You can attack with a flurry of multiple elbows as you work your way through the attacker's hands and forearms on the way to his chest, throat, or face, and then reverse the process as you work your way out.

GRAPPLING

Other than foot sweeps, you won't see many grappling techniques in karate tournaments. Can you imagine applying a come-along hold on an opponent's arm? It would get a laugh, but few competitors are going to chance such a move.

I once saw a competitor execute a beautiful over-the-shoulder judo throw in a karate tournament. His opponent was a very aggressive fighter who loved to charge with a flurry of hand techniques. On one occasion when he attacked with his flurry, the other fighter caught his extended arm,

If you can get an arm free, elbow him in the jaw.

pivoted, slammed his hip into the man's lower midsection, and executed a high, over-the-shoulder throw. He immediately followed with a body punch and earned a point. Luckily, the thrown man was not injured.

It's been several years since I saw that move, but I still remember it vividly. It was a wonderful example of the "art" in martial art, a perfect blending of karate and judo. The throw was acceptable in this case because the opponent was not injured from the fall, although he easily could have been.

With the high cost of tournament insurance and the ever-present risk of lawsuits, many tournaments now forbid takedown techniques. The risk of cracked heads or broken arms is too great a possibility. If the sport is to survive, there have to be strict safety rules.

There are no rules on the street; the only thing you want to survive is you. If a grappling technique fits the situation, use it. If the attacker hits the ground a little too hard, too bad. He made the choice to attack you; you choose how you want the situation to end.

The grappling arts — which include jujutsu, judo, aikido, wrestling, and chin-na — are devastating. There are holds, locks, pins, takedowns, chokes, and bone-breaking techniques that can cause misery, injury, and death.

In training, you know immediately whether or not your grappling technique is working. When you apply a hold on a finger, you get instant feedback as to its effectiveness, especially when your opponent is writhing in agony. On the other hand, the result of a karate technique is always open to conjecture, unless you hit your opponent full force.

It would be ideal to study a grappling art in conjunction with karate, but cost, time, and other restrictions limit most people from studying two arts. A good alternative is to familiarize yourself with a few grappling techniques that are simple, realistic, and applicable for close fighting, especially in a clinch.

It is advisable to learn two grappling techniques against an attacker's head, arms, and legs — areas susceptible to takedown techniques.

The basic principle when attacking the head is: where the head goes, the body follows.

Technique 1. From a clinch, grasp the attacker's hair close to his scalp, preferably one hand on each side of his head. Curl your fingers into a tight fist and jerk his head downward. Step back and take him to the ground.

Technique 2. Interlace your fingers behind your opponent's neck. It is paramount for you to point your elbows downward as you jerk his head downward. If your elbows are pointed out to the side, the technique will be weak. Pull his head

Grasp his hair and jerk his head downward. From here you can knee him or pull him to the ground.

into a knee smash or pull him all the way to the ground.

When attacking the shoulders, the principle is: tilt the shoulders and the body follows.

Technique 1. As the attacker leans his weight into you and clinches, grasp the clothing at the front of his shoulders and tug him forward and downward. Remember to point your elbows downward.

Technique 2. As the attacker leans to the right or left, use his clothing to pull his lowest shoulder down while simultaneously lifting underneath his other arm. If you are taking him to your left, for example, swing your left leg to the left as you turn your body to the left. You can move your leg and rotate your body as much as 180 degrees, thus creating a strong momentum to take the attacker down easily.

The principle for attacking the legs is: weaken the trunk and the tree falls.

Technique 1. When in a clinch, slam two or three kicks into the attacker's shins. Fake another. When he starts to lift his foot to avoid your kick, sweep it aside the instant his weight comes off of it and pull his shoulders in whatever direction he falls to take him down.

Technique 2. When you are both upright and not leaning

From a clinch, pull down on one shoulder, lift under the arm, and pull/push him to the ground.

into each other, hook your upper calf behind his closest knee and pull it toward you. As his balance starts to falter, push his upper body in the direction he is leaning.

Obviously, your attacker is not going to make it easy for you to do these techniques or any others that you attempt. Grappling works best when there is an element of surprise — a sudden and perfectly timed movement. Also, remember that it's okay to hit him to weaken or distract him prior to the application of the grappling technique.

Hook his left knee with the back of your right knee and pull him down.

5 Sparring

Today, it is good business for a school to claim it teaches street self-defense. I have noticed, however, that fighting styles that claim they are street-oriented practice sparring the same way tournament styles do, with an emphasis on the all-important point. The result is that even well-meaning streetfighting styles end up playing karate tag during sparring. They move in and out of range, zapping one another with a limited number of techniques aimed at a limited number of targets, then raise their fists in victory and exhibit all the other nonsense that would get them hurt on the street.

Some styles practice tournament sparring because the instructor doesn't know anything else to teach. This is often a result of one generation of black belts passing their knowledge and teaching approach on to the next. Teachers teach what they have learned. This chain is only broken if someone questions the concept and begins to explore alternatives.

SPARRING AND REAL FIGHTING
One of the first things I learned as a military policeman was that real fighting seldom occurs like karate sparring. I

witnessed and was involved in lots of streetfights, bar brawls, assaults, and resisting-arrest situations, events I continue to be involved in as a city police officer. It's been my experience that most fights consist of a sudden flurry of techniques, then it is over. Few go on for two or three minutes, as in competition. There are exceptions, of course (before I began training, I was in a fistfight that lasted twenty-five minutes), but typically the skirmish is over after a quick exchange.

Sparring has its place in a street-oriented style, but it is conducted differently because it has a different function than tournament sparring. Mentally, your objective is to do what you have to do to survive, as opposed to tournament sparring, where your goal is to garner points. On a physical level, street-style sparring allows you to experiment with a wider variety of techniques, because in the street, anything can be used.

MENTAL APPROACH

During street-oriented sparring, the thought of hitting an opponent only to earn a point must be replaced with a total mental commitment to stop an attacker from hurting you. You must be willing to hurt, seriously injure, or even kill him.

When practicing street sparring, don't think in terms of rules, fair play, good manners, or acting like the perfect lady or gentleman. This is because by the time you are actually physically engaged in a real fight, you will have already exhausted all passive ways of avoiding it. You will have tried to talk your way out of the situation and tried to find an escape route. If these failed, or if you had been jumped or in some other way attacked, you had no choice but to fight. Once the fight has begun, you must be mentally committed to use whatever techniques or means available to protect yourself or someone else.

You must think only in terms of survival and you must fight with a controlled rage that has no limitations. You must think about breaking joints, gouging eyes, pulling hair, and breaking limbs. Do not think about two-minute time

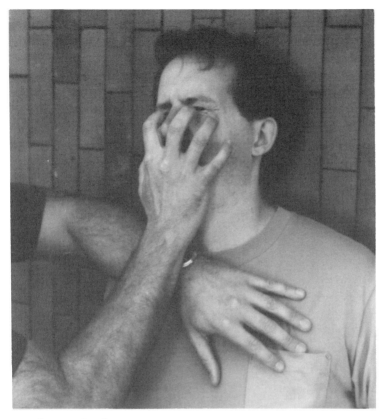

Do whatever it takes to survive.

limitations, drawing the judges' attention to your techniques, dazzling the crowd, or impressing lovers or fellow students. Also — and this is the big one — do not think about what the rules allow and disallow. Your only objective is to survive.

PHYSICAL APPROACH

On the physical level, street sparring is easier than sport sparring and a lot more fun. You can do *anything*, including things you would never attempt in sport karate, as long as it is effective at stopping the opponent.

For example, when your opponent throws a kick, catch

it and hit the leg with a punch, kick, knee, or elbow and, before you release it, kick his support leg several times. If your sparring partner keeps his guard close to his body, execute controlled punches and kicks at his arms. Repeated kicks and punches to his biceps and forearms and strikes to the back of his hands with your knuckles would, in a real fight, take a toll on his ability to cover and protect his body.

Below are a variety of sparring exercises that will prepare you physically and mentally for street survival.

Light-contact sparring

Contact sparring is a fun drill designed to mentally and physically desensitize you against getting hit. As the name implies, this sparring drill requires that you make light contact with all of your punches and kicks. Protective equipment is worn so you will not get hurt but can still feel the impact. The eyes, groin, and knee joints are extremely vulnerable to even light contact and should not be considered a target in this exercise.

Contact sparring is especially beneficial for students who exhibit great fear toward getting hit. Although this is usually seen with new students, veteran students can also be hesitant, especially if they have been training in a style that does not allow contact.

When you first begin light-contact sparring, it is best to make contact only to the body to give yourself time to get used to the idea. Move around with your training partner in the usual sparring fashion and exchange blows to the chest, arms, back, abdomen, thighs, and calves. Although you are probably used to only using your feet to attack lower targets, experiment with punches to the legs, especially the easier-to-reach upper thighs. You will be surprised how accessible the legs are to hand attacks.

The next step is to make light contact to the head. Unless you are wearing a face shield, blows to the neck and fingers to the eyes are too dangerous and should not be allowed. If you are especially sensitive about face contact, try this drill first. While wearing safety hand gear, face your partner and exchange taps to the cheeks, chin, forehead, nose, ears, and back of the head. Although you may begin this drill with some anxiety, you will probably end up having a good time with it.

Some students become desensitized after one session, but others may take longer. It doesn't matter how long it takes as long as you keep working at it until you get results.

The final stage in contact sparring is to spar as you normally do, but be free to hit any open target (other than those mentioned as being too dangerous). Although harder blows to the head are potentially unsafe, some students may want to advance to medium-hard blows to the body and legs. Your goal is to immediately counter after you have been hit and not give the contact any significance by reacting to it.

There are many stories of experienced karate people getting psyched out after getting hit hard in a real confrontation. They had not trained for contact and, when struck, were unable to function. Can you imagine a boxer acting this way? Of course not. He expects to get hit and to continue fighting. How you train is how you will react in a real fight. When you take a blow, give one back.

Contact sparring is a fun drill that benefits both fighters. One person experiences the feel of making contact, while the other learns to take a hit and immediately give one back. Too many people lose a fight because their minds shut down after they have been hit. You must train to develop an attitude that the fight is not over once you have been punched or kicked. Train to continue fighting until your last breath.

Hitting only the legs

If you train in a tournament style, kicks and punches to the legs are probably not allowed since they are not allowed in competition. In the street, however, kicks to the leg muscles and joints can easily end a confrontation in seconds.

In order to implant into your mind the concept of attacking the legs, you need to include leg strikes in your training.

An easy but effective exercise is to spar, but make the legs the only target you can hit with your punches and kicks. Use all the same ploys as in your regular sparring — fakes, combinations, tricky foot work — but strike only the legs. Go for the inner thighs, back of the thighs, knee joints, calf muscles, ankle bones, Achilles tendon, and the top of the feet.

With just a little isolation practice, you will be amazed how quickly you will begin thinking about the legs as a viable target area. If you have an occasion to have a friendly sparring session with someone from another school, you will be pleasantly surprised how easy it is to hit them in the legs and how difficult it is for them to block your techniques.

Hitting only the arms

Have you ever received a hard blow on your arm and immediately experienced an intense, shooting pain followed by a numbness to the limb? This is a common injury in karate that usually forces the recipient to stop training momentarily, sometimes longer. When the muscles and nerves have been injured, the arm loses its effectiveness.

Blows to the arms are not awarded points in tournaments but they definitely count in the street. Unfortunately, few karate students give them consideration as a viable target, primarily because their training has been directed at hunting for tournament point areas.

As with any new concept, you must first implant in your mind the idea of hitting the arms. As with the leg-hitting exercises, a fast way to properly condition your mind is to spend a part of your sparring sessions making the arms the only target. You will find it difficult to hit your partner's arms when he knows what you are going to do. But that will get you thinking even more, because you will have to develop effective strategies in order to hit them.

In a streetfight, consider punching the bicep muscles and striking the elbow joint. Injury to these two targets will affect a fighter's ability to bend his arms. Think about striking at

A solid punch to an attacker's arm won't earn a tournament point, but it can immobilize his arm.

the hands, specifically the fingers, to cause acute, debilitating pain and injury. It's hard to be aggressive when a jammed finger is sending electric bolts of agony all the way to the shoulder. If you can grab your opponent's wrist, execute hard blows with your other hand to his forearm muscles, which will cause a numbing sensation up his arm.

In training, you should wear padded hand protection and control your blows. Your frame of mind, however, is that you are actually injuring these targets. Never just toss a technique at a target. Know why you are striking it and the subsequent injury potential. The arms will now be part of your overall target selection, thus giving you more places to hit, rather than the limited targets associated with sport karate.

A word of caution: since the arms are vulnerable to injury from excessive contact, you and your partner need to monitor the degree of impact, especially blows to the elbow joint.

Moving into range

There are three ranges in which you fight. Range 3 is the kicking range, where most karate students feel the most comfortable. Range 2 is the punching range, where the hand specialists like to work. Range 1 is the close-fighting range, where some karate students feel comfortable and judo and jujutsu students shine. You have spent time perfecting individual techniques in each range; now you are ready to put them together to overwhelm a street attacker.

The concept of moving into range involves starting with a Range 3 technique, flowing into a Range 2 technique, and then into a Range 1. For example, attack with a roundhouse kick, backfist, and elbow. The flow is smooth, fast, and powerful because you are building forward momentum. It can also have the psychological effect of overwhelming an attacker. The attacks are coming fast and furious, making it difficult for him to set up a defense or counter.

In this drill, you and your partner should not block each other's techniques. You want to think only about moving through the ranges without having your techniques stopped or deflected. Work on developing speed and smoothness so that your techniques blitz your opponent, leaving him feeling helpless. Once you and your training partner feel comfortable with the concept and have explored a number of techniques, begin working the movements into your regular sparring.

Moving out of close range

Tournament competitors rarely think about close-range fighting. This fact is especially noticeable when they spar, because they quit attacking as soon as they get in close. For example, a typical tournament fighter will attack with a roundhouse kick, backfist, and reverse punch combination as he works himself in close. He then stops his attack and moves out of range. He retreats without hitting because the exchange is over and, in sport karate, it is unnecessary to do anything else because the judges are scoring the attack.

How you train is how you will react in a real fight. A good

On the street, there won't be judges to break up your clash. You will need to work your way out by smashing him with a close-range technique . . .

streetfighter is not going to let you out of range so easily. Once he has you in that close and you are no longer attacking, he will take advantage of your position.

It is imperative that you develop a habit of continuing to fight as you move out of range. Realize that if you are not hitting, your assailant probably will be. Anytime you are within hitting range, you need to fill the time with kicks and punches so he is on the defensive rather than you.

As you are sparring, be cognizant of keeping up a continuous barrage of techniques as you are moving into range. As you

. . . a middle-range technique . . .

move out of range, reverse the process you used moving in. That is, use close techniques as long as you are close, hand techniques when you have moved back to hand range, and kicking techniques when you are at leg distance. A classic attack would look like this: Range 3-2-1-2-3. Of course you can add as much as the situation allows in each range, such as 3-3-2-1-1-2-2-3. Fill all the ranges with offensive techniques to keep the attacker too busy to do anything. Remember, when you are within range, he can hit you, too. Therefore, get to him first.

. . . and a long-range technique.

No-block sparring

Sparring without blocking is a fun drill that is beneficial for tournament competition and street self-defense. The primary difference is that when training in street sparring, you can hit any target you want.

As the name implies, you and your opponent spar without blocking each other's attacks. The drill is designed for success; everything you do works. As a result, you are free to execute attacks you might otherwise be hesitant to attempt. You get to see all of your attacks completed without having them blocked or jammed. You can even combine the concept of no-block sparring with contact sparring, hitting with light to medium contact.

Impairment sparring

When you get hurt in training or competition, you stop sparring and give the injury attention. This is a natural response since you are not fighting for your life, and it's important to check the injury to see if further training might be detrimental.

On the street, however, you do not have this luxury. Can you imagine calling time to an attacker as you hop around holding your foot and rubbing an injured toe? Of course this would never happen. If you received an injury, you would have to keep fighting and tend to the injury later.

Impairment sparring is an excellent exercise that lets you examine what you can and cannot do when you no longer have all of your weapons. Without a left eye or a right arm, you must alter your attack and defense to accommodate the limitation.

Impairment sparring works this way. As you are sparring with your partner, take turns telling each other what the other's injury is. For example, tell your opponent, "Your left eye has been injured." He then closes his eye and you continue sparring. After a minute or two, tell him his injury has healed, and then spar normally for another minute. Then it's his turn and he says, "Your left hand has been injured," and you spar for a couple of minutes with the new limitation.

Use your imagination and give your opponent an assorted array of injuries. This is a popular exercise that is not only fun but beneficial.

Statue

Statue is an exercise that helps train the eyes to see targets. The concept calls for both sparring partners to freeze motion so targets are more visible and there is time to decide how to hit them.

The exercise is performed this way. You and your training partner decide who is going to be A and who is going to be B. Begin sparring at slow to medium speed. A third person, usually the instructor if it is a class exercise, calls out, "statue!" and you and your opponent freeze in place. The instructor then calls out one of the letters. The fighter called upon attacks.

What the attack is and how the opponent reacts depend on how the exercise is set up. For example, the response can be that you attack your opponent's legs as he remains like a statue. Or the attack can be a combination, where the recipient is allowed to block only the first blow, thus simulating a reaction to a fake, and allows the second attack to hit an exposed target.

The basic concept in the statue exercise is that time stops so the attacker has a moment longer than normal to determine the best strike. He must determine, based on his opponent's frozen position, what target to hit and what weapon to use. If the students are beginners, targets and specific attacks should be limited so they have only one or two choices to make. Experienced fighters are allowed a broader choice unless they are working on a specific concept.

A fun variation of statue is to execute a takedown technique when your partner freezes. No matter what position your opponent freezes in, you must take him down using a leg sweep or some other type of grappling technique.

Using the statue drill is one of the best ways to grasp a sense of disrupting an opponent's balance, even if you have had little, if any, training on specific takedown movements. The drill will help you develop an eye for detecting where your opponent's balance is strong and where it is weak and vulnerable for a takedown. For example, if his weight is on his front foot and he is leaning slightly forward, that is the direction you want to take him. Move in quickly and execute the most applicable sweep.

If you are unfamiliar with sweeps and jujutsu techniques, you can experiment with other ways to take an unbalanced opponent down. When statue is called, study your opponent to determine the easiest way for him to fall. If he is leaning back over his rear leg, simply give him a nudge in that same direction. This can be done by pushing against his shoulder, pulling his hair, yanking his arm, or tripping him.

With practice, you will be able to see instantly when a person is vulnerable for a takedown. Of course, circumstances will not always allow you to take advantage of the situation, but when you are able to, you will do so with a greater understanding of what it takes to upset a person's balance.

Statue is a good interim drill between learning the mechanics of a takedown and applying the movement during sparring. It is more realistic than practicing from positions that are staged and ideal because the positions in the statue exercise flow out of natural sparring movements.

Cluttered and cramped spaces

Your school training takes place in a large open space. Obstacles such as gym bags, shoes, punching bags, and other training equipment are kept to the side. This is done to keep the training area unobstructed so training can be conducted safely, without concern of tripping or falling over anything.

In competition, sparring matches are held within a square ring, also kept clear of obstruction. In fact, judges are always reminding the competitors on the sidelines to keep their feet out of the ring. As in the school, the concern is to maintain a clear area for the fighters' safety.

In the street, you do not always have a choice of deciding

where you will defend yourself. It could be in the wide open space of a parking lot, where you are able to move freely and execute an assortment of techniques. More than likely, however, it will be between parked cars or some other cramped area, where your movement will be dramatically curtailed.

For a real learning experience, try sparring in a cluttered space.

For years I have practiced in open spaces, yet the majority of my physical confrontations have been in small, cramped places. In the course of my police career, I have been in fights on stairwells, boat piers, and roof tops, and in closets, phone booths, and public restrooms. I can recall one unpleasant experience when I had to defend myself against an enraged drunk in a small, slippery, stinking, skid-row restroom, where the toilet and urinal had been overflowing for several days.

Examine sparring in places other than your school training area, such as your school locker room or basement. Sparring in cramped and cluttered spaces is enlightening because it exposes you to a realistic environment and forces you to adjust your fighting techniques. During your sessions, litter the floor with objects you normally keep aside. It's fun and it's a challenge for the whole class to spar around gym bags, chairs, papers, sticks, or anything you can toss out into the training area.

Training in your basement with a friend is also interesting. You will immediately discover there are some techniques that are impossible to execute and others that need to be modified in order to be functional in the cluttered quarters. For example, you will find it hard to kick your opponent when he is on the other side of a pile of boxes and you will discover that executing a normal reverse punch is difficult when your back is pressed against a wall.

Multiple attackers

Tournament stylists train with and compete against only one opponent. In a street situation, there is a good chance there will be more than one attacker, since bullies and other street vermin rarely act alone. They need their courage fortified by having a cohort nearby who they know will back them up.

Sparring with two opponents will expose you to the difficulty of having to divide your attention when you are attacked from all directions. You will have to learn how to employ your techniques and position yourself when you are under the added pressure of a second opponent.

Your practice doesn't have to always involve two opponents attacking you. On the street there may be two adversaries, but that doesn't necessarily mean both will be punching and kicking at you. One subject may be urging the other on, with an occasional push or punch when you come close to him. He may not be as active as the other, but you still have to consider him a threat because you don't know to what extent he will become involved.

Put together a sparring exercise where one opponent is fighting you while the other circles and harasses verbally. He may throw an occasional punch or kick when you come close, but his job is to divide your attention and hit at you sporadically. A variation is to have opponent A stop sparring with you, then opponent B attacks while A encourages him.

Create your own scenarios in order to add realism and strategic thinking. Experiment to see what works and what doesn't. Discuss the results with your training partners and teacher and watch as your concept of realistic sparring improves.

No matter how skilled you get at this exercise, never attempt to fight more than one attacker if you have the option of escaping. If you have the misfortune of facing multiple attackers who pounce all at once, you will most likely lose, no matter what your belt rank. Successfully fighting off a mob of assailants only happens in karate movies.

Blind sparring

As we have mentioned before, most karate training and competing is conducted in ideal environments while streetfighting takes place in less than ideal places. One such condition rarely addressed in training is the issue of lighting. While your school and competition area is well lit, real fighting will often occur at night in locations that are lit poorly or not at all, such as hallways, alleys, parking lots, parks, basements, and so on.

Blind sparring is conducted as follows. With your eyes open, grab your opponent by his arm, shoulder, or uniform front. Now, close your eyes and attack your partner with punches, kicks, and close-quarter techniques. Your opponent keeps his eyes open and blocks only a few of your attacks, occasionally executing a counter just to make the exercise more realistic and a little harder for you.

Your first objective is not to let go of the opponent as you hit and grapple with him. If you lose contact with an assailant in a dark room, you will be in a weak position; you don't know where he is or what he is going to try next.

Your second objective is to take him to the ground. You can have your opponent simulate reacting to your blows and slowly drop to the floor as you hit him with a barrage of techniques. Or you and your opponent can agree that only a grappling technique can be used to get the attacker down. Push your head into his shoulder to avoid getting punched in the face. Clinch to avoid his long-range techniques while you keep your elbows and knees hitting and pushing. Trip and grapple for a takedown and then hang on for the ride as he falls. Continue to hit him on the ground until the drill has been halted.

Since techniques are thrown blindly, it is important that caution be used to prevent excessive contact. Be sure to wear protective equipment and, although your eyes are closed, employ as much control as possible.

Fighting for real without vision is possibly the worst situation you could be in. If your assailant is armed, say with a knife, you wouldn't know it until you felt the steel slice into your body. It would then be imperative that you maintain contact with him and fight to control his arms. If you can determine which hand holds the knife, control that hand and force the knife into his body, if that's what it takes. Find his throat and choke or strike it, or put your knee across it if he is on his back. Find his eyes and jam your fingers into them. Find his groin and squeeze or strike it with all your strength. You are in a fight for your life, and you must do whatever it takes — including the use of deadly force — to survive.

"Blind" sparring with your eyes closed will help develop your awareness in darkness as you punch, kick, and grapple your opponent to the ground.

*　*　*　*　*

Street sparring should always be kept realistic. Always ask yourself if you would use this technique against a 220-pound street creep who is trying to rearrange your facial features.

Never say "yes" too quickly. Take the time to analyze the technique to determine its strengths and weaknesses. Ask yourself:

- Does the technique have stopping power?
- Does it leave me open?
- Can I flow into another technique from it?
- Is it a point-getter or will it really stop an attacker?
- What are the best targets to hit in this situation?
- Are there any excess movements I can omit?

Defensively, ask yourself:
- Will this block really stop an attack?
- Is this the best block for me, given my size and strength?
- Does the block leave me open?
- Can I counter quickly after the block?
- Is this the fastest block I can do in this situation?
- Can I evade quickly enough to avoid getting hit?

6 Vulnerable Targets

I have been training in the martial arts long enough to have experienced just about every type of injury. I have been punched and kicked by tournament fighters and I will quickly admit that most of the blows hurt. But few blows were so painful that I couldn't have continued fighting if the situation had been a real fight.

I have also received injuries over the years that were so debilitating that I was unable to continue to train or compete. Had the injury occurred in a real fight, my will would have been sapped and I would have had a difficult time defending myself. Interestingly, few of these injuries were to targets that would have earned a point in competition. Instead, they were accidental techniques (or so my opponents claimed) that fractured a finger, gouged an eye, or broke a kneecap. These are acutely vulnerable targets. The injury not only caused intense agony but also destroyed my will to continue.

In a tournament, you are not concerned with specific targets because you are striking only at those broad areas that will earn points — the head and the upper-body. In a streetfight you can't depend on tournament targets to stop an attacker. A punch to the upper chest, back, or forehead will hurt, but

124 ■ Anything Goes ■ 124

will the pain be sufficient to stop a determined aggressor bent on hurting you? Or will he be so psyched he will ignore the pain and continue his assault?

In tournaments, the most vulnerable targets are off-limits and the most deadly techniques are either illegal or never recognized as legitimate points. Targets such as the eyes, elbows, fingers, thighs, knees, ankles, and Achilles tendon are illegal, and such techniques as eye gouging, hair pulling, face clawing, ear ripping, ankle stomping, and muscle pinching will probably get you disqualified or thrown out of the tournament. In the street, however, it is these techniques that will save your life.

When your tournament is over, it is important that you train to hit all targets. If you get into a habit of mentally defining targets as those that are legal and those that are not, you may find yourself hesitant to hit an off-limits target in a real fight. When fighting for real, there is no time for hesitancy; you must be able to react to an opening instantaneously.

DESTROY THE ATTACKER'S SPIRIT

This is my rule: if you destroy the man's spirit you will destroy the man. You do not always have to enter a fight with the intention of knocking the guy out or killing him. The former may never happen and the latter will get you into a lot of trouble. However, if you think in terms of diffusing his spirit, the situation may end a lot faster and a lot easier.

One of the definitions of spirit, according to *The New World Dictionary*, is, "Vivacity, courage, vigor, enthusiasm." In order to attack you, the typical street thug will have one or more of these qualities. When you take away one or more of these, you take the fight out of the man.

Along with diffusing an attacker's fighting spirit, you also want to cause him pain. I have found that the more acute the pain, the quicker the fight leaves the man. A finger flick to the eye will do more to take the fight out of an attacker than the average point-getting reverse punch to the body.

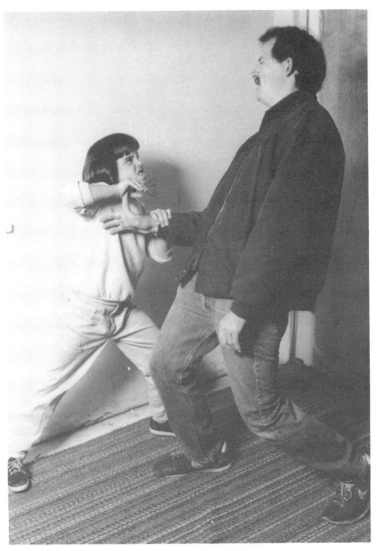

Even a child can break an attacker's spirit by pitting her strength against a vulnerable target.

A roundhouse kick to the stomach of a big man might hurt him or it just might make him mad. Instead, slap your hand hard across his Adam's apple or grab his little finger and break it and watch the fighting spirit ooze right out of him. When you take an attacker's spirit in such a manner, he will stop bothering you and you can bet he will always remember you.

Most of the techniques listed below are illegal in tournament competition. They are debilitating and they will cause acute pain, two factors that will sap the spirit right out of a fighter. It's one thing to experience the dull ache from a punch to the chest and quite another to have a fist slammed against a locked elbow joint. The chest blow hurts, but the elbow strike sends a laser beam of burning pain straight to the brain — and the psyche.

Most of these targets and techniques will never be seen in competition because they are extremely dangerous. Some may even seem brutal. But if you cannot avoid the fight and the situation becomes life threatening, then it's nice to know how to be brutal.

Hair

Twisting the hair causes excruciating pain to most people. There are two methods to apply hair techniques. One is to simply grab a handful of hair and pull, an excellent tool to assist with a takedown technique. This next method is the most painful because it involves twisting the hair at the roots, an area where the nerves are quite sensitive. Grab a handful of hair on each side of the attacker's head, clutching all the way to the roots, and jerk your elbows downward. Twist his hair downward and continue to twist as you step back and take him to the floor.

Ear

A hard blow to the ear creates a sound and sensation in the brain similar to a small explosion. It can have a disorientating effect and cause tremendous pain throughout the skull. Any punch or kick to the ear is effective, especially if the attacker is down, with one side of his head on the ground. Tearing, clawing, slapping, and biting the ear are also effective techniques.

A hard elbow into the ear will cause an explosion of pain in an attacker's head.

Eyes

Here is a simple principle: if a guy can't see, he isn't worth a darn in a fight. It's true the eyes are hard to hit because they are small and the head is mobile, but if you can get at them, you probably will end the fight quickly. Use all five fingers to claw, rake, jab, or slowly push into the eyes.

Many fighters are too squeamish to attack the eyes for fear of causing blindness. Unless you thrust a finger deep into a socket, you are not going to cause permanent damage. You will, however, cause the attacker to panic and clutch madly at his face, at which time his will to continue his attack will stop.

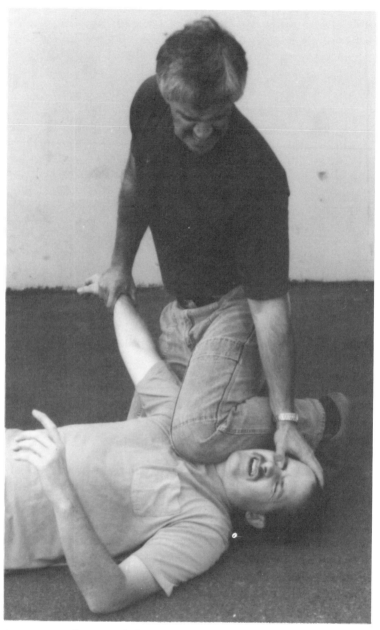

Gouge a man's eye and the fight will ooze out of him.

Nose

Although it's a fallacy that you can drive the nose bone into the brain (it's not a bone), you can still take a person's fighting spirit away by smashing his nose with a hard kick or punch. If the attacker is down and the back of his head is supported by a wall or floor, more force will be absorbed by the target. Even if you hit lightly, his eyes will water, which will affect his vision and allow you to hit him at will.

You can also jam one or more fingers into his nostrils and twist or tear. It is extremely painful, disconcerting, and can give direction to a takedown technique.

Neck

A hard blow to the front of the throat can kill. A less forceful blow will cause a choking sensation, setting off panic. A chop to the back of the neck, as corny as it looks in the movies, will cause a tremendous explosion of pain throughout the head. I once slapped a man across his Adam's apple and he dropped like a two-hundred-pound sack of potatoes. It's a vulnerable target that will drain an attacker's spirit in a second, but be careful because it is potentially deadly.

Upper arms

The biceps, on the front of the arms, and the triceps, on the back of the arms, are surprisingly vulnerable. Repeated punches to an attacker's biceps will disable him in a short time. Upon impact, the tender muscles are slammed against the bones, injuring the tissue and the nerves, subsequently making it difficult or impossible to lift the arms and clench the fists.

If the attacker has fallen and his arm is stretched out on the ground, a powerful stomp to the upper arm will take the fight right out of him. Additionally, grinding your knee or shin into his biceps or triceps when he is down will cause pain and immobilize him.

Stomping his upper arm will squash his tender biceps muscle against the bone, taking away his will to fight.

Elbow

Once the attacker is down on his stomach, apply pressure against his elbow with your hand or knee to prevent him from moving. Or execute a knee drop or foot stomp on his elbow to cause severe trauma to the joint. Even if he can get up, he will be in so much pain he will be unable to continue fighting.

When the attacker is standing, direct punches and kicks at his elbow joint. When the arm is bent, the blows will cause pain and possibly injury; when the arm is straight, the pain and injury will be even greater. Have you ever bumped your elbow against a hard object and experienced tingling and numbness throughout the entire arm? Imagine what a full-powered punch or kick delivered against the elbow joint would feel like.

Fingers and wrist

These are small targets and a little difficult to hit, but if the opportunity presents itself, kick and punch them hard in an attempt to jam or break the bones. The pain is so intense, it may render the entire arm useless.

Let's say the attacker assumes a boxer's fighting stance. Immediately snap a backfist into the back of his lead hand, making contact with your two large knuckles. If the blow is hard enough, it may render his arm useless or, at the least, distract him and provide you with the opportunity to hit him elsewhere. Since both of your hands are involved with this technique, your delivery must be fast. You must be on guard as to what your opponent is doing to avoid a counter from his other hand.

If you can get a hold of his hand in a grappling situation, use the side of your other hand to chop his wrist. Strike at the ulna nerve, located on the little finger side of his wrist, or against the radial nerve, located just below the base of his thumb. Both points cause numbness and will cause him to drop any weapon he may be holding.

You can also grab a finger and break it by jerking it back.

If the attacker is down, stomp on his fingers, wrist, or the back of his hand. A fighter's spirit diminishes when he can't use his hands because of pain and injury.

Upper body

Personally, I never think of the upper body as being an effective target. In most parts of the country, it is padded with a heavy winter coat eight months out of the year, making it difficult to penetrate with punches and kicks. Also, since it is a large target, most fighters, even untrained ones, will make some attempt to keep it covered with their arms.

There is a lot of literature that says a hard blow to various upper-body targets will paralyze or kill an attacker. This may be true, but incidents of this occurring are very rare. Of the millions of people practicing martial arts and boxing, it would be a logical assumption that there would be a lot of paralyzed and dead people since all fighting arts include body blows. But there are not. Does that mean everyone is doing a good job of pulling their blows? I don't think so.

I have been training since 1965 and I know of three people who have died while practicing. Two were in competition and one was working out in his school. All three had physical ailments that existed independent of their karate; their death happened by chance while they were practicing.

In order to kill or paralyze someone with a body blow, the situation has to be so ideal as to make it virtually impossible to purposely preplan. On those rare occasions when it has occurred, it has been by chance only. This is because various elements have to exist, such as speed and power of the technique coupled with body momentum and precise body positioning of both fighters. The recipient's breathing pattern must be at its most vulnerable and the target must lack muscle tension. There are other factors as well, but the bottom line is that the conditions must be ideal.

If I may say so, I deliver a pretty powerful punch. Nonetheless, I have had occasions when the guy just looked at me or ignored me altogether after receiving one of my best shots (being ignored hurts the ego the most). There have been other times when my seemingly easy blow resulted in a knockout and, in one frightening situation, caused a heart attack. On either end, I didn't plan on being ignored and I certainly didn't plan on giving a man a heart attack. The conditions and elements of those moments combined to create the result.

I am not saying to never hit the upper body. I am simply suggesting that you not walk around thinking that if you hit someone in the liver, he will automatically die. The result is happenstance. He may ignore you or double over in pain. The chance of him dying, however, is quite remote.

There are six targets in the upper body that, when hit with sufficient force, will help diminish an attacker's fighting spirit. Use these targets not so much as an end but as a distraction on the way to the more vulnerable targets discussed in this chapter. Don't even bother with them if the attacker is wearing a heavy coat.

Nipple

A blow to the nipple hurts. If the attacker is bare chested or wearing a light T-shirt, a fingernail claw to the nipple will cause acute pain. Punching or kicking it hurts because the chest muscles underneath are tender. If the attacker is lying on his back and you execute a hard kick or punch to the nipple area, the pain will be even greater because his body will absorb all of the impact.

Solar plexus

A blow to the solar plexus, located just below the chest and just above the stomach, can knock the wind out of an attacker, which is one of the fastest ways to take away fighting spirit. A punch or kick to the solar plexus will cause sufficient pain and distraction to enable you to follow up with additional techniques. Stomping the solar plexus when the attacker is on his back can be deadly.

Liver

A hard blow to the liver, located on the right side of the body behind the ribs, will weaken a fighter and sap his energy. Roundhouse kicks with the left leg are effective, as is continually pounding it with a left roundhouse punch. If he is lying on his stomach, hard kicks to the liver will make him want to stay down.

Ribs

I survived a rough-and-tumble year in Vietnam only to have a training partner break my ribs with a side kick my second day back home. The ribs are quite susceptible to being broken, and there is always the danger of a rib puncturing a lung. If you deliver the blow to the lower part of the rib cage, the attacker will probably get the wind knocked out of him.

Kidneys

The kidneys are located on both sides of the body near the back. Hard kicks and punches to the kidneys are painful and can weaken the body immediately. The pain feels as if the organ is being squeezed in a clenched fist. I received a hard kick to the kidneys once and urinated blood for over a month.

Stomach

A hard blow to the stomach will knock the wind out of a fighter and, consequently, diminish his fighting spirit. For maximum results, take him down on his back and stomp or jump on his stomach.

When standing, the recipient of a hard stomach blow will bend at the waist and drop his hands to cover the impacted area, making him vulnerable for follow-up techniques. Since his upper body is leaning in an off-balanced position, he is also vulnerable for a takedown.

Groin

For most people, men and women, the groin is an extremely

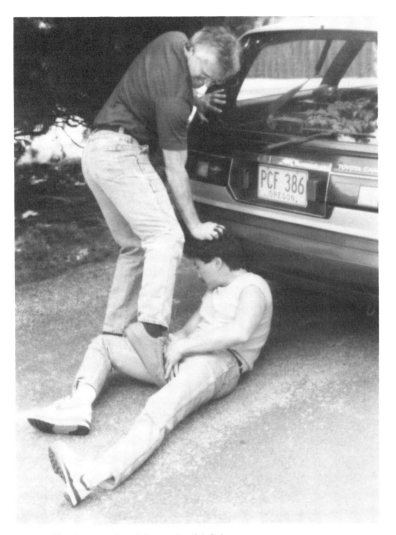

Even if he is covering his groin, kick it anyway.

vulnerable target. There are some people, however, who can withstand a strong kick or punch to the groin and keep on fighting as if it had never happened. Such people are rare, but they are out there.

The old standbys are effective: kick, punch, grab, and

squeeze. If the attacker is lying down, a kick or stomp is a good finishing technique.

The attacker's natural reaction is to drop his hands and cover his groin. Just because you have struck the groin once doesn't mean you can't hit it again, even if he has it covered with his hands. Just as getting kicked in the groin while you are wearing a protective cup hurts, punching or kicking an attacker's groin through his covering hands will still cause pain.

Thighs

Kicks and punches to the large muscles of the thigh not only hurt but the pain sends a shock wave throughout the entire limb. Deliver the blows to the center of the leg so the impact will drive the muscle against the thigh bone. Striking the back of the thigh will cause some pain, but the front and sides are the most vulnerable to pain. Once the leg starts to weaken and the attacker takes his weight off of it, move in quickly and execute a leg sweep. If the attacker has fallen onto his back, execute a powerful stomp straight down onto his thigh.

Knee

With training, you should be able to deliver many times over the amount of force it takes to break a knee joint. Front, side, and back kicks against the kneecap are best for breaking. Circular kicks work well for causing shock, distraction, and debilitation. You can strike to any side of the knee. Once it has been injured, move in and sweep the leg out from under the attacker.

Shin

The shin has very little covering to protect its nerves. Straight-in kicks work best and can deliver enough impact to cause pain and debilitation, especially when kicked by a hard shoe.

Calf

The calf muscle is quite tender, especially the center of the broadest part of the muscle. Use the tip or the hard edge of your shoe to deliver front and side kicks to the muscle. If the attacker is on his back, execute a stomp or a knee drop onto his calf.

Ankle

Like the shin, the ankle has very little meat covering it for protection. Although the entire area is vulnerable to a kick, contact with the protruding bone on the outside of the ankle is especially painful. If the attacker lifts his foot in agony, push or sweep him to the ground.

If you are in a grappling situation and have hold of the attacker's foot, try to sprain his ankle by twisting it hard in either direction.

Stomping the Achilles tendon will cause great pain.

Achilles tendon

The Achilles tendon is located above the heel and below the ankle. Impact to it can be debilitating and may cause permanent crippling. Straight kicks work best. If the attacker is on his stomach, a knee drop to the Achilles tendon will finish him.

Foot

The top of the foot and the toes have many small bones that are easily broken. Stomps work best.

7 Using the Environment

In this chapter we are going to take a look at the arsenal of weapons that surround you wherever you may be. Additionally, we will examine how you can use such things as walls, cars, trees, and other fixed objects to your advantage.

BEING AWARE OF YOUR ENVIRONMENT

As a martial artist, your training should make you more attuned to your environment and more prepared for the unexpected than the average untrained person, who most often walks around completely oblivious to his surroundings. Just sit in your car downtown and watch passersby. Most of them are so wrapped up in where they have been or where they are going that they are not paying any attention to where they are at the moment! In police work, we view these people as victims looking for a place to happen.

If you are mentally aware, you are at a higher level of alertness than the average person. You are cognizant of your immediate surroundings and, without being paranoid, you are aware of everyone to your front, back, and sides. You are quick to perceive the way people are acting, walking, and standing together. You can easily evaluate the mood of a bar, a group of people standing on a corner, or drinkers at a party. On the outside you will appear to be relaxed and cool, but your brain will be evaluating data continuously.

This is not paranoia but rather keen observation and the weighing and screening of information as the brain receives it from the eyes. In fact, you should be able to carry on a conversation, have a good time, and go about your business without anyone being aware of what you are doing. Watch a police officer sometime, especially one walking a beat, and you will notice that his eyes are always moving, taking in everything, while the officer goes about his routine business.

Some people call this awareness a sixth sense. Bruce Lee argued that there is no such thing — rather it is a sharpening of the existing five senses. This is closer to the truth. When you are completely aware, you are using all of your senses to monitor your environment, consciously and unconsciously analyzing all input, disregarding that which is nonthreatening, and focusing on anything out of the norm.

You must realize that a threat or physical attack can happen anywhere at anytime. It can happen while you are eating in a fast-food restaurant, using an automatic bank teller machine, or opening your car door. It can happen when your hands are empty, when you are fumbling with your car keys, or carrying an armload of groceries.

Often times, students are taught to drop whatever they have in their hands so they are not encumbered in their defense. This isn't always necessary because no matter what martial art you study, with a little imagination and creativity, you can turn whatever you have in your hand — coffee cup, credit card, key — into a weapon that will add surprise and effectiveness to a variety of techniques.

This is not to say you would deliberately go into a situation with one of these weapons held at the ready. But if you were shopping and you were suddenly attacked while you were pulling money from your wallet, you could use your wallet to surprise counterattack your assailant by flipping it in his face and then following up with a punch or kick. Never think

This woman uses her handbag as a weapon to thrust into an attacker's throat.

of an object in your hand as a hinderance to defending yourself because it can often supplement your techniques.

Look around and note the potential arsenal within reach. That pen in your pocket can be used to gouge a face, scrape a cheek, or press against a sensitive nerve. The soda pop can you are holding will add authority to a hammerfist strike or, when thrust into an attacker's face, cause enough distraction to allow you to execute a foot sweep or slam a hard kick into his groin. A lightweight jacket whipped about might confuse an attacker and the zipper could lacerate his face. There are similar weapons in your car, office, schoolroom, grocery market, and laundromat.

In today's society, you cannot carry such weapons as nunchaku, ninja spikes, whip chains, or staffs. It would be inconvenient, not to mention difficult — how inconspicuous would you be carrying a seven-foot staff? Additionally, our judicial system does not like you to carry them, and they especially don't like it when you use them on people, no matter what the situation.

Although these weapons have historical significance in the martial arts, they were designed for fighting and killing, and the court system will look at them in exactly that light. On the other hand, combs, keys, and coffee cups are not designed for fighting and are not viewed as dangerous weapons by the courts. The exception would be if you were to use them excessively in your defense — that is, beyond what the situation required.

PRACTICAL APPLICATION

How do you incorporate these weapons with your karate? The first answer is that it depends upon the circumstances of the specific situation. You must evaluate your predicament to determine what technique is the most applicable, given the particular weapon you have in your hand. If you were in a check-out line with your wallet in hand when you were attacked, your response would be different than if you were attacked while seated and drinking a cup of coffee.

A child can use a schoolbook to add authority to a thrust to the face.

Secondly, the basis of any self-defense situation is simplicity. Always rely on the basics. As we have discussed throughout this text, keep the flashy techniques for demonstrations and the basics for the street. Besides, just how fancy can you get with a car key?

For the next several days, look at objects around you as potential weapons. If you are at home or your karate school, physically experiment with objects to see what can be done with them. You will learn that a coffee cup can be thrust into an attacker's abdomen like a punch, smashed against a cheek like a backfist, swung into the groin like an uppercut, and brought down on the back of the head like a hammerfist. You will be amazed at how much damage a rolled magazine can do when it is whipped across the eyes, smacked against the side of a neck, used to strike a hand holding a knife, or thrust into a groin.

Cramped behind this desk and seated on this chair, one might think I am at the mercy of an attacker. Not so. Can you imagine how my attacker would look with an imprint of the alphabet on his face after I smash him with my computer keyboard?

Practicing with assorted objects is not only fun, but your confidence level will rise when you begin to realize you are surrounded by an arsenal of weapons.

USE THE ENVIRONMENT TO YOUR ADVANTAGE

There is a scene in Bruce Lee's *Enter The Dragon* where he is on a ship en route to a martial arts tournament. A bully who has been antagonizing him challenges him to a fight. Bruce tells him that he will fight him using the art of "not fighting."

When the bully asks what he means, Bruce tells him to get into a row boat and they will go to a nearby island, where he will demonstrate the art to him. The bully agrees and climbs into the boat. Bruce, using the environment to his advantage, does not get in. Instead he lets the boat's rope uncoil so the bully and the boat trail far behind the ship for the rest of the journey.

While driving in Portland one day, a motorist pulled alongside me and abruptly cut me off, nearly hitting my fender. I honked my horn, a response he apparently took as a challenge to fight. He immediately started playing little games with me: swerving his car toward mine, tailgating, and motioning for me to pull over. Looking ahead a half block, I saw something I could use to my advantage.

He was on my passenger side as we pulled to a stoplight, again waving at me to pull to the side of the road so he could teach me a lesson or two about honking. I nodded that I would oblige. As the light changed he roared forward and cut over two lanes to the side of the road. At this point he realized I was in a left-turn lane. As I made my turn onto the freeway ramp, I could see him cursing in my rearview mirror as three lanes of traffic prevented him from following.

These are two examples of using the environment to avoid fighting. Bruce Lee could have defeated the bully but chose instead to defeat him with his wits. If I had pulled over and fought my freeway acquaintance, I could have been attacked with a crowbar, a gun, pushed into traffic, or I could have beat him to a pulp and been arrested. Motioning for me to pull over was not an attack and, therefore, the situation was not self-defense. If I had pulled over and a physical confrontation occurred, it probably would have been judged as mutual combat in court and I would be wide open for a lawsuit if I'd hurt him. Instead, I used my environment to my advantage and made him feel stupid.

In a tournament, you are deliberately going into the ring to engage in battle. Your intent is to fight. But in the street you want to avoid fighting for the same reasons I didn't pull my car over to confront the troublemaker. The risk is too great to agree to a mutual combat situation because it's a risk whether you win or lose.

KEEP YOUR AVENUE OF ESCAPE OPEN

Never get yourself into a position where the troublemaker

is between you and an avenue of escape. When you sense a potential problem, immediately look for a way to physically remove yourself from it. Avoid getting yourself trapped into a corner.

For example:

- Cross the street when you see a suspicious person or persons on the sidewalk ahead of you.
- Walk into a business if you think you are being followed.
- Park on the street rather than in a dark parking lot.
- Move to the far end of the subway car if you think there is going to be a problem.
- Sit with your back to the wall so you can see what is going on in a bar.
- Look to be sure everything is okay inside a convenience store before you get out of your car.
- Sit as close to the bus driver as you can.

CREATE A PSYCHOLOGICAL ADVANTAGE

This is a little trick I learned as a police officer. I'm 5'11", and there are lot of taller bad guys. I like to create the illusion that I am taller by standing on the curb when they are standing on the street. If they are on the sidewalk, I try to stand on a step. If I am talking with someone on a stairwell, I will stand on a higher step. This is a subtle technique, but it creates an illusion of size that in some cases may be all it takes to make someone think twice about causing trouble.

CREATING REACTION TIME

Action is faster than reaction. This is an important principle in physical combat because even good fighters can get hit if they are not cognizant of an impending attack.

If you are standing within striking range of a potential assailant and he initiates an assault, he will have already gone through the thinking and planning process. You, however, are suddenly in a position of having to react to what he has already planned. As his fist is rushing toward your face, you need to see it, your eyes need to send a message to your brain,

Stay greater than arm's reach from a threat to give yourself time to react.

and your brain needs to react and send a message to your muscles to block or duck. If you are standing too close, you will not have enough time to react defensively.

To give yourself time, stand farther than arm's reach from any threat. This forces an attacker to take a step or two to bridge the gap in order to hit you, providing you with a moment longer to react.

By using objects from your surroundings, you can add even more time to your reaction. As a police officer walking a beat a few years ago, I was constantly approached by drunks and mentally ill people. I would often position myself so there was a parking meter between me and the potential threat. There were many occasions when a person would lunge for me and I would just step back and watch him confront the meter. Not only did I avoid the initial attack but the parking meter gave me a little more time to formulate a quick plan.

Other objects you can use to increase your reaction time include fire hydrants, trees, lampposts, traffic signs, sidewalk displays, cars, bar stools, and grocery store food displays. But be aware that such objects can also pose a threat to you, especially if you don't know they are near. Don't be caught by surprise. Preplan so that these objects are a problem only to your attacker.

Below are listed a few ways you can make your environment hazardous to an assailant's health.

- Position yourself so he has to look into the sun or any other bright light.
- Move toward him so he has to back up toward traffic.
- Push him down a set of stairs.
- Push him over a fire hydrant.
- Slam him into a brick wall.
- Kick a chair into his legs.
- Throw a drink into his eyes.
- Throw dirt or sand into his eyes.
- Slam your car door into his body.
- Push him into a phone booth and close the door.
- As you run out of a restroom, shut off the lights.

MENTAL PREPARATION

Mental preparation is the process of visualizing a situation so you will react more smoothly should a similar situation actually occur. Instead of reacting with surprise and awkwardness, you will react with the experience gained from having been in a similar situation before, even if it was only in your imagination. Studies have shown that visualizing an event will give you close to the same benefits as having actually experienced it.

As you go about your day, take a few seconds to imagine

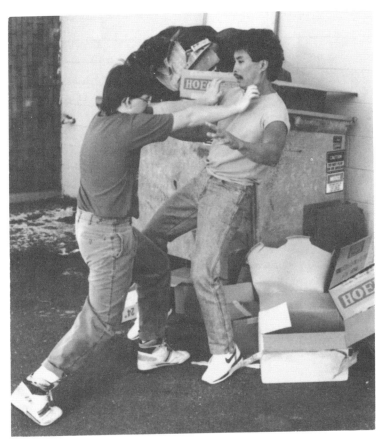

Use the environment to your advantage.

various scenarios. As you are pushing a grocery cart down an aisle, imagine a couple of thugs rounding the corner and coming at you. What would you do? What can you use that is within reach? Can you imagine the effect a can of dog food would have slammed against a creep's temple?

As you are walking down a street, imagine there is a young punk sucking from a can of beer, watching as you approach. What would you do? If he were to attack, what could you use for a weapon? How could you use your environment?

Visualizing situations like these need not take any longer

than a few seconds. No one is aware that you are entertaining thoughts of great battles. The visualization process helps to develop an awareness of your environment and how you can use it in a self-defense situation. It's something you should do only on occasion and for only a few seconds at a time.

BE SUSPICIOUS

Police officers are always observing their immediate surroundings and the people therein. When someone approaches an officer, his eyes scan the person as a potential threat, a process that takes place in an instant. The person's hands are observed first, then a quick scan of the body, especially the waist, where weapons are often hidden.

If the approaching person is an elderly woman, the officer's evaluation is made quickly and unconsciously. If the person is a street punk with metal-studded wrist braces, swastika tattoos, and spiked purple hair, the officer's evaluation is going to be on a conscious level. The person's mannerisms and other actions are going to be observed more intently, and he will continue to be observed until he leaves the officer's area.

It can be argued that a police officer needs to be suspicious since that is the nature of the job. You, however, are a law-abiding citizen who just wants to go to school or work and not have to be suspicious of everyone. This is certainly a reasonable expectation. Unfortunately, the climate in our large cities today does not allow us to walk around with our heads in the clouds. Those that do usually find their names on police reports as victims of theft or assault.

We do not have to live in a state of paranoia. We do have to be alert and occasionally suspicious, and we do need to have a plan.

8 Some Thoughts About Fitness and Stances

You don't have to be in good shape to fight in tournaments, and it's a good thing because most competitors are in terrible condition anyway. I have seen nationally ranked fighters who presented an overall appearance of poor fitness: big bellies, poor endurance, and a lack of flexibility. They did well in competition, however, because they had learned how to win at the tournament game.

Streetfighting is not a game, and good fitness, especially good endurance, can mean the difference between winning and losing. I have found that even when my endurance is at its best, I will still be winded and tired after struggling with a resisting suspect. If I am not in my best shape, a struggle will leave me coughing, wheezing, and completely exhausted.

A real fight presents a different emotional commitment than school or tournament sparring. Suddenly finding yourself in a self-defense situation will cause stress and fear, which have a direct effect on your breathing pattern. Your inhalation and exhalation will be rapid and shallow and you will hold your breath, especially if the fight turns into a contest of strength versus strength. Stress and fear will tighten your muscles, causing your breathing to become erratic, sapping your energy, and dissipating your strength.

Whether you are fighting in competition or defending yourself in the street, physical and mental tension are common elements you must contend with. You can lessen the intensity, however, by training to be in top physical condition. Boxers and wrestlers know this and train hard to be in the best shape for their competition.

Karate students should always be in top condition in order to survive an all-out street self-defense situation, to compete at their best, and to present the best possible image to the public. There is no excuse for an experienced student, especially a black belt, to walk around with a protruding belly and huff and puff after a few minutes of mild training.

To be in top mental and physical condition, you need to develop and maintain three aspects of physical fitness.

STRENGTH

It is true that the martial arts were developed in Asian countries, where most people are of a relatively small stature. It is also true that small martial artists are often capable of amazing kicking and punching power, a power that derives from a combination of specific body mechanics and high-velocity movement. It has been my experience, however, that students who include strength-developing exercises in their training are better for it. I have also found when two students are of equal rank, experience, and knowledge, the physically stronger will usually dominate.

For years there has been a belief that weight training will slow one's movements. There is some truth to this when a person develops his muscles to a size indicative of a heavyweight competitive body builder. When muscle size is far beyond the norm, there is a good possibility that movement will be restricted.

I have trained with weights for many years and, in fact, I at one time competed in physique competition. Although I had pretty good size when I was younger and have a little above-average size now, weight training has never hindered

Leg extensions will build power into front and roundhouse kicks.

my martial arts ability. Over the years, I have taught several students who also trained with weights regularly, and there was never a problem with their ability to perform karate movements. In fact, all of the students I have had who have developed a muscular physique have also developed into excellent martial artists. Perhaps as a result of their weight training, they were more in tune with their bodies and, therefore, able to learn quickly how to coordinate their mind and body in the martial arts.

I encourage you to supplement your karate training with strength-developing exercises. If you have access to weights, follow a sensible training regimen. If weight training is an impossibility, you can develop a good level of strength through free-hand exercises such as push-ups, sit-ups, slow kicking, and muscle tensing. (See my book, *The Way Alone: Your Path To Excellence in the Martial Arts*, also published by Paladin Press, for an excellent weight-training program and numerous free hand exercises.)

FLEXIBILITY

Most karate systems recognize the necessity of flexibility and, therefore, include stretching exercises in their warm-ups. The problem is that most of us should do more. If the exercises are not a formal part of the training, many students do just enough to loosen their legs a little and then begin kicking and punching.

Not only does this lackadaisical approach to stretching invite injury to the muscles and joints, it does not improve the student's range of motion. Increased flexibility can only be achieved through regular stretching exercises designed to work the legs, hips, back, waist, arms, and numerous smaller muscle groups.

There are several advantages to greater flexibility:

Increased kicking speed

Increased flexibility means less restriction in the muscle fibers and less restriction in the joints. The motion is carried out smoothly, quickly, and almost effortlessly. A person who has achieved a high degree of flexibility will have legs that seem to move almost independently of the body. Kicks can be executed without telegraphing and without extra body assistance, such as tucking the chest or bobbing the head.

Greater flexibility will lessen the chance of injury and increase speed and power.

Less chance of injury

Many leg injuries occur as a result of poor flexibility. When a leg or lower back is made to move beyond its range of motion, a tight muscle will be strained. This can result from kicking too high, slipping on the floor, fatigue, insufficient warm-up, and any of a variety of awkward movements. A strain can range from momentary discomfort all the way to a muscle tear that will require surgical repair.

The greater your flexibility, the less chance you will be injured. Although you can't always help or predict awkward or overextended techniques, increased flexibility will help decrease the chance of experiencing one of those surprises.

A self-defense situation will not provide you with an opportunity to warm up. It may occur after you have been walking in freezing temperatures for a couple of hours or while waiting for a bus on a cold, windy street corner. You won't have time to warm up because you will be too busy blocking and hitting.

Cold weather slows your blood circulation, which stiffens your muscles and joints. When you go to throw that super kick you possess, you will be surprised how slowly your leg responds to your mental commands. Good flexibility will not keep you from getting cold and stiff, but you will have more range of movement before the cold and stiffness restricts your muscles.

ENDURANCE

The dictionary defines endurance as the ability to last and continue, and to stand pain, distress, and fatigue. These attributes are exactly what you need to survive a streetfight, especially if it lasts longer than two or three minutes. If you poop out when you are defending yourself, you may go home carrying your head in a basket.

It is important to include endurance training in your regular workouts. I am a firm believer that the endurance workout should be the same activity as the activity you want to be fit for. I am always amused by students who say, "Gee, I'm out of shape for the tournament coming up. I better start jogging."

The benefits of jogging may not help your endurance for the martial arts. Some people benefit from it while others do not. Additionally, many students complain that their muscles tighten and their kicks become less fluid when they jog. It's true that boxers and wrestlers do a lot of roadwork for endurance, but when was the last time you saw a boxer throw a sidekick?

Design your endurance training to fit the activity for which you want endurance. If you are a kata competitor, practice kata over and over with little or no rest in between. If you are a tournament fighter, spar nonstop. By using karate as your endurance exercise, you are not only building your heart and lung strength, you are also improving your karate.

You don't have to go out and pick fights to improve your streetfighting endurance. This would only get you in trouble, and you would really get out of shape in jail. You can use kata, sparring, high-repetition kicks and punches, bag work, and any of the many drills and exercises discussed throughout this text to prepare you for the rigors of a streetfight.

The activity should be carried out for at least fifteen to twenty minutes to get the minimum strengthening effect for your heart and lungs. It has to be nonstop and at a pace that elevates your heart rate to about 75 percent of its maximum. A simple formula for determining your maximum

157 ■ Some Thoughts About Fitness and Stances ■ 157

heart rate and your training heart rate is as follows:

$$220 - 20 = 200 \times 75\% = 150$$

Take the base number 220 and subtract your age; let's say you are 20 years old. That makes 200 your maximum heart rate. If you are already in pretty good shape, you should train at 75 percent of your maximum heart rate. Multiply 200 by 75 percent, which gives you a training heart rate of 150 beats per minute. If you are out of shape, you should start at 60 percent and gradually, over a period of several weeks, progress to 75 percent.

This is not a situation where more is better. It has been found that training at a higher percentage will not improve your endurance and can actually be detrimental. If you feel you need more, increase your training time to thirty minutes or longer, but do not go over 75 percent of your maximum heart rate.

Determine your heart rate by checking your pulse on your neck or wrist. Count the beats for six seconds and multiply by 10. This will provide you with your heart rate for one minute. If you are supposed to be training at 150 beats per minute and your reading was 120 beats, you need to pick up the pace a little. If your reading was 170 beats per minute, you need to slow down.

Remember, never stop your training longer than the six seconds it takes to get your reading. You need to keep going in order to keep your heart rate elevated.

Include endurance training in your workouts at least three times a week. Your endurance will improve, you will look and feel better, and if you should ever have to defend yourself in the street, you will improve your chances of winning.

STANCES

There are some fighting arts, especially traditional styles, that use stances that are impractical and even detrimental in a streetfight. Many students of ancient Japanese, Okinawan, and Chinese systems would argue this point, but most likely they are people who have never tried to use these static and stylized stances outside of their schools.

At the other extreme are fighters who use weak stances or virtually no stances at all. They stand too high, don't cover themselves, face their opponents straight on, lack stability, and move around without any apparent design to their footwork. Their fighting ability is ineffective because their foundation is weak.

It is not uncommon to see tournament fighters square off with each other and then remain frozen in their stances for several seconds as they "feel" each other out. Perhaps they have read stories of Japanese masters who squared off in competition and remained frozen in their stances for over an hour waiting for the right opportunity to attack. Sorry, folks, but that ain't going to work on the street.

Never assume a deep, motionless stance against an attacker. You should never stay in one place for more than a few seconds. You should be in constant motion, moving forwards, backwards, sideways, and circling. By doing so, you will make it difficult for the attacker to land an accurate blow.

You are a hard target to hit when you're moving. When an attacker tries to move in, you are no longer there. It is difficult for him to time his technique and to judge distance when you are in one place no longer than a second or two.

On the other hand, it is easier for you to land a successful blow when you are in motion because it is difficult for the attacker to see your initial move. If you pose in a deep, classical stance for thirty seconds and then attack, your initial movement will be easy to detect.

Professional full-contact karate fighters learned right away that the old stances do not work. You will never see them use a low, static back stance or a low horse stance with their buttocks three inches from the floor. Instead, they employ stances and movements that are virtually the same as boxing. They are in constant movement, shuffling and bobbing as they exchange offensive and defensive techniques. Since there is hard contact and potential for a knockout, the fighters have had to make stance changes for the sake of survival.

This deep, traditional stance would not offer mobility against a fighter who is circling and moving quickly in and out of range.

I am in no way comparing full-contact kickboxing to streetfighting — at least 80 percent of karate's techniques are not allowed in the sport — but since they are trying to hurt each other, it is a step closer than point fighting.

I let my students discover the best stance for them. There are some styles, especially traditional ones, that teach all students to use the same stance. This is wrong. Contrary to their teaching, it is not important that the student adapt to the style; instead, the style should adapt to the student. Height, weight, physical structure, strength, speed, and skill are all important in determining a student's choice of stances.

There are, however, some basic characteristics that should be considered when developing your stances. On offense, your feet should be a little wider than shoulder width. Your knees are bent far enough to give you an explosive spring; if your stance is too high or too low, your mobility will be slowed. You are not static in this position; you are moving around, watching for an exposed target, and trying to keep your opponent confused as to what you are doing. The width and height of your stance will fluctuate as you move, which is okay, as long as you keep in mind the general guidelines mentioned above.

On defense, assume a slightly wider stance to increase your stability. In a streetfight, no matter how skilled you are, you will probably get hit with a punch or kick. If your stance is strong, you can receive the blow and not get knocked off balance or knocked down. Your upper body should be rotated slightly away from the attacker so you present less of a target.

Your arms should always be on guard and offer cover for the upper body. The basic posture is to hold your rear hand near your solar plexus and your lead hand extended with the arm bent at about forty-five degrees. As with the feet, the arms should also be in motion, but in such a way as to always provide protection. When you lower your front arm to cover your groin, you should raise your rear hand near your chin. When you lower the rear hand to the area of your waist, you should raise your front hand to give protection

With your knees slightly bent and your feet a little wider than your shoulders, you are able to move quickly in any direction.

Defensively, your stance should be a little wider and lower so you have greater stability against a strong attack while still being able to counter quickly.

to your head.

Being mobile does not mean you are jumping around and waving your arms madly about. All movement is done with purpose: to evade, confuse, set up an attack, and hit when it is least expected. Your steps are short so you are never caught spread out and exposed. Do not cross your feet unless you are out of range. Then, just when the attacker has determined that your style is to move around continuously, stand motionless for a few seconds. This will confuse him and lull him into making an error.

Standing in a static stance against an attacker armed with a knife or pipe may be the last mistake you ever make. Do not become a bowling pin waiting for the ball to hit you. Move quickly and erratically and as soon as the opportunity to escape presents itself, take it and *run*.

Natural stance

Some assaults happen so quickly, you may not get the opportunity to assume any type of stance. You should occasionally train using a natural, upright position, as if you were standing on a street corner reading the paper when you were attacked.

Practice all of your hand techniques, offensive and defensive, while standing in a normal position. Examine how they feel without body momentum and hip rotation to assist in their execution. Examine your kicks. How powerful is your sidekick without the momentum generated from lunging toward the opponent? What are the easiest kicks to deliver from an upright, casual position?

Seated

Few karate schools consider self-defense in a seated position, although is it not uncommon for people to be assaulted while sitting in a bus, subway, movie theater, park bench, or even in their own cars. Remember, street thugs prey on people they think are weak and in a defenseless position.

Would you really want to use a deep, static, traditional stance against this attacker?

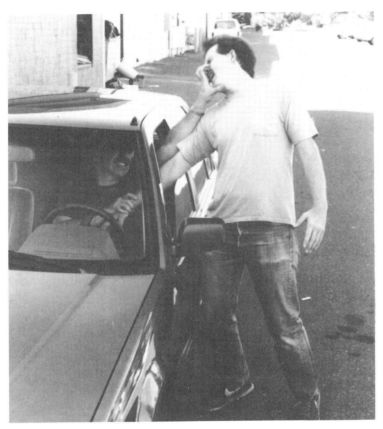

Use your car in your defense. When the attacker reaches for you, grab his arm, slam it down on the window, and finger rake his eyes.

There are no special techniques to be used from a seated position, but you do need to examine what you can and cannot do. Experiment to see what kicks are effective, given the limited amount of movement you have. Are the knees and groin the best targets available? What are the best targets to hit with your hand techniques? Is grappling an option?

Consider using your environment. How about hitting the attacker with the chair? Also, experiment with holding onto the chair or bench for added support when delivering your attack.

One last cheap shot

If you have been practicing a traditional style for a long time, you will have a hard time recognizing the impracticality of your stances, and you will certainly find it difficult to make the necessary changes. I have found traditionalists to be the most closed-minded when it comes to improving the martial arts.

If the fighting arts are to progress, we must continually examine them with a critical eye and an open mind. Stances are one area that need to be evaluated continually. Those styles that have recognized the need to change have improved.

About the Author

Loren W. Christensen began studying the martial arts in 1965. He has been teaching karate since 1967 and holds black belts in jujutsu (1st degree), arnis (1st degree), and karate (5th degree). He has been rated as a top-ten kata competitor three times and has written five books and dozens of articles on the martial arts.

Christensen has been a police officer since 1967. He has taught police defensive tactics to many law-enforcement agencies and has developed instructional programs for the police straight and side-handle batons. He has also taught defensive tactics to many private security agencies, college law-enforcement classes, and private organizations. Christensen is an expert witness in court cases involving martial arts weapons and the use of empty-hand physical force.